I dedicate this book to little dreamers, who find in the colorful pages a universe where their imaginations can fly freely. May this work bring joy, learning and many magical moments. With affection, [Sandro]."

Sandro Geovano

2024

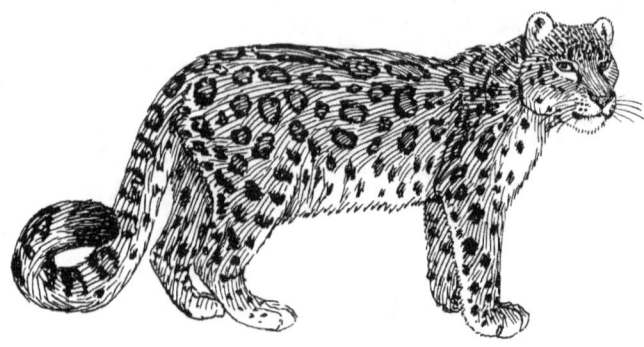
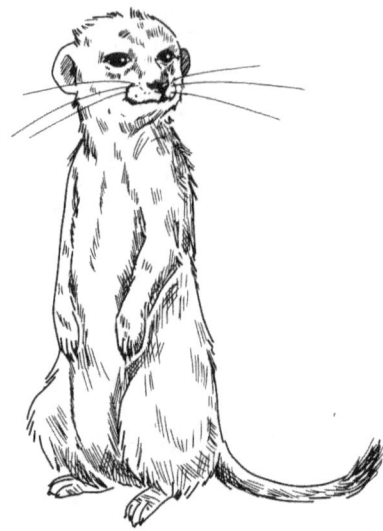

This Book Belongs to:

○——————————————————————○

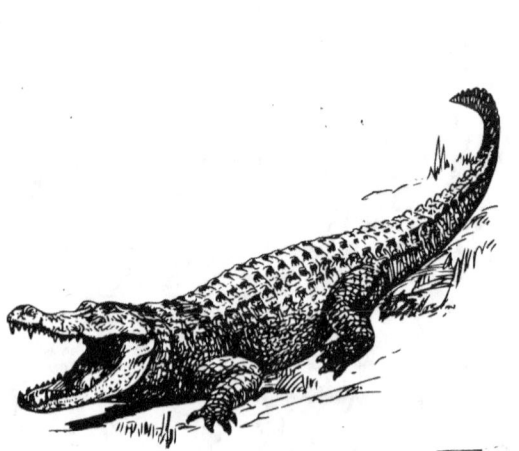
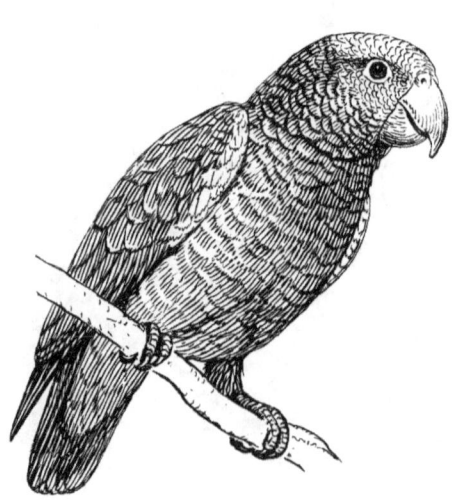

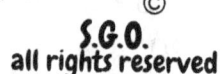

Test Color Page

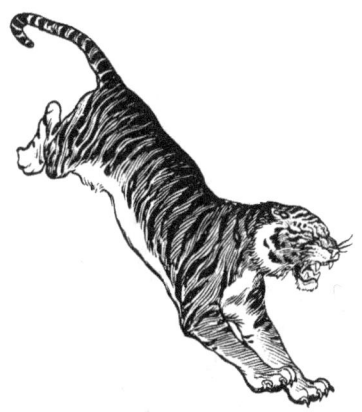

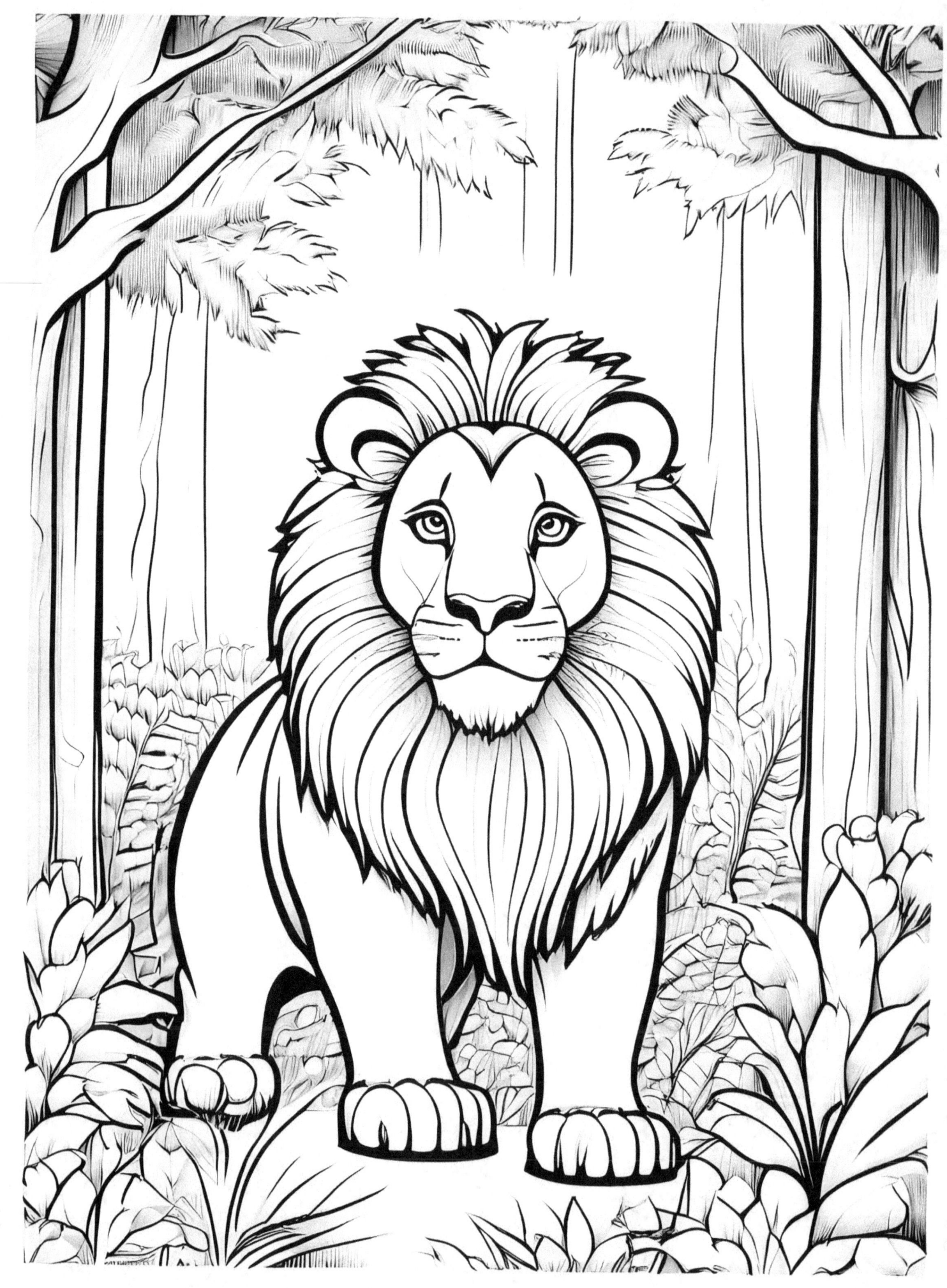

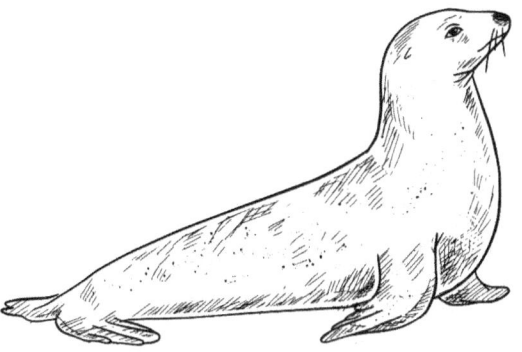

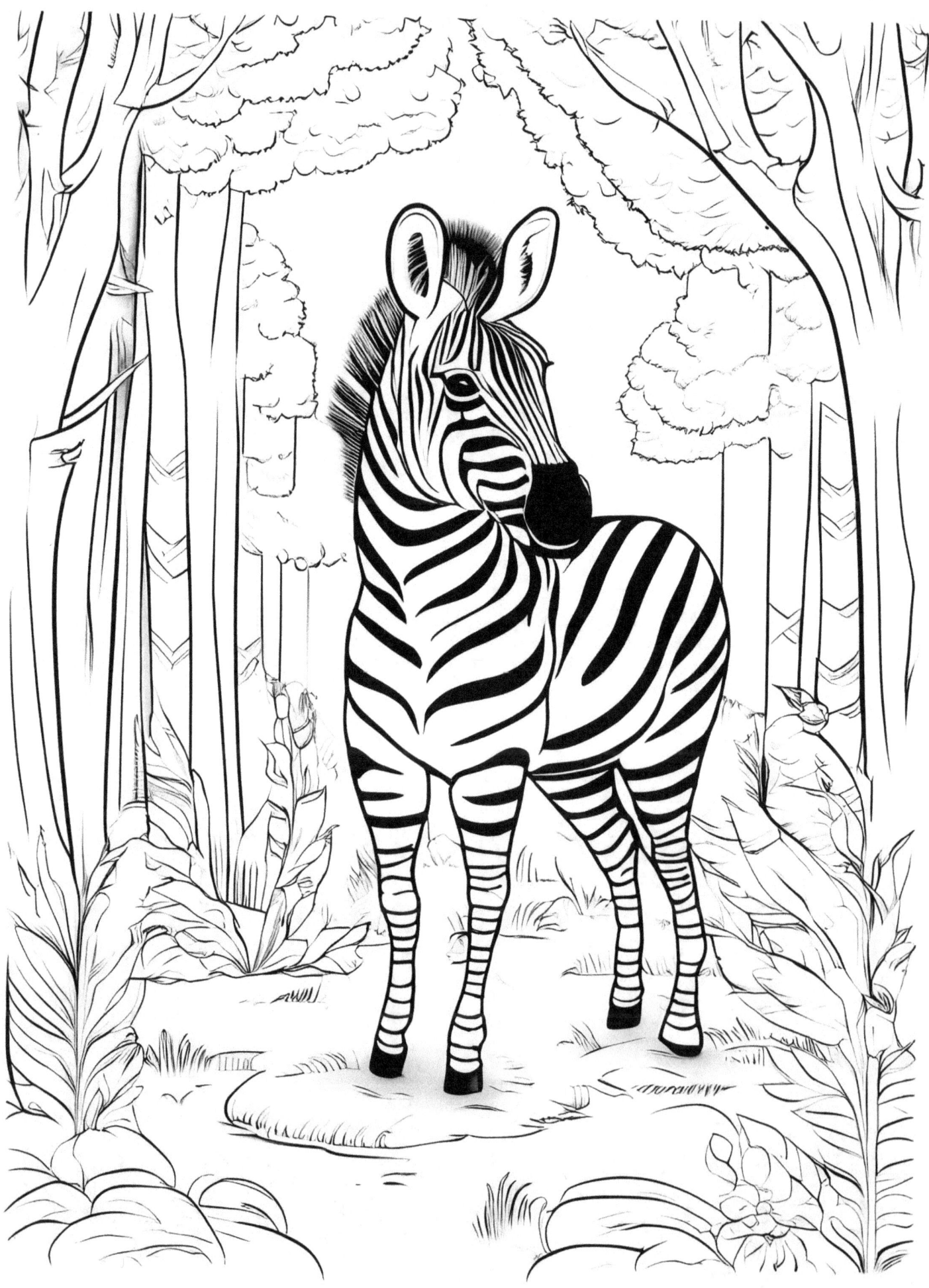

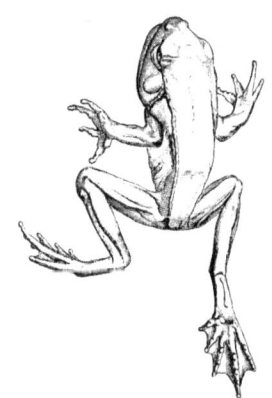

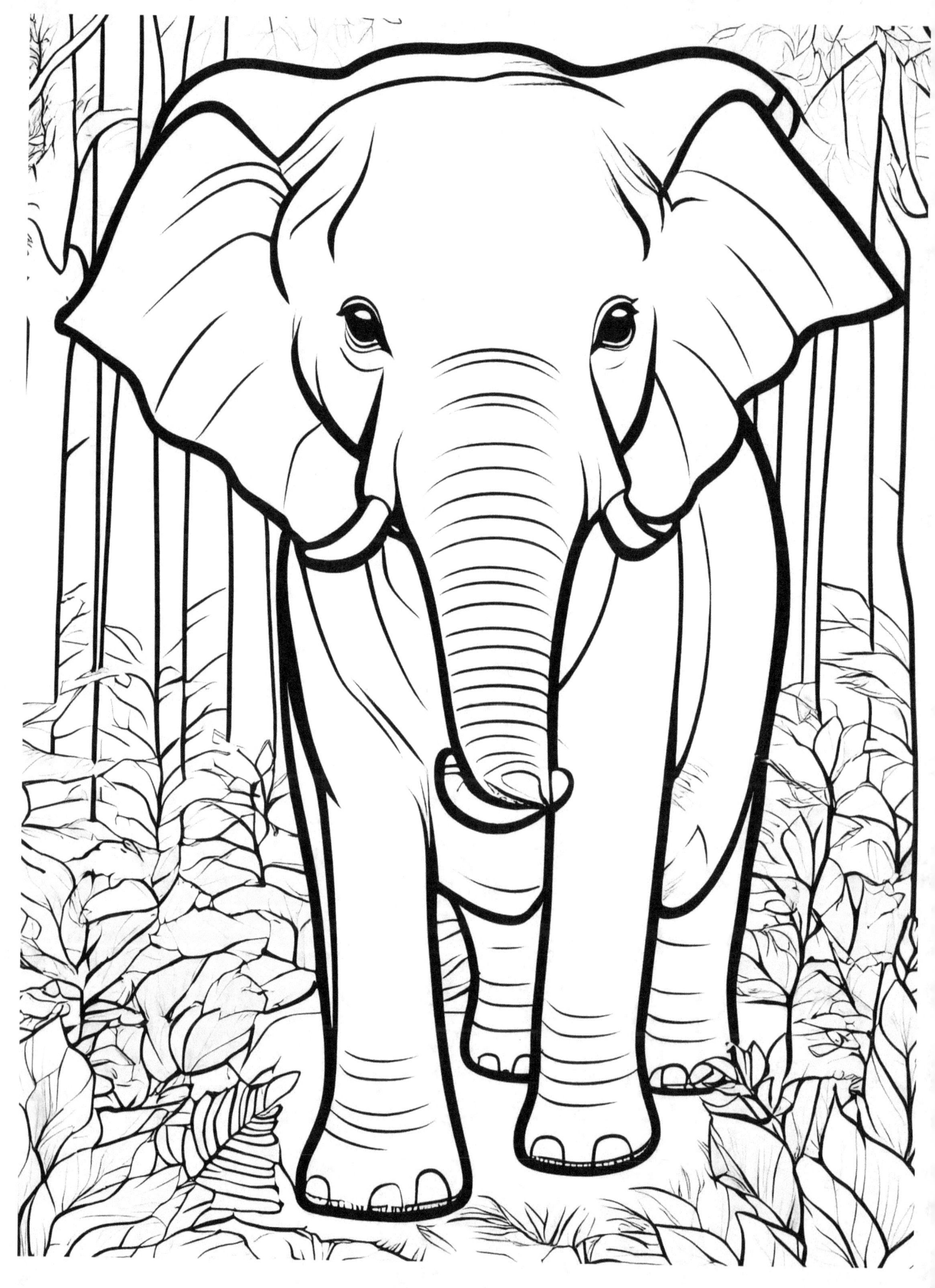

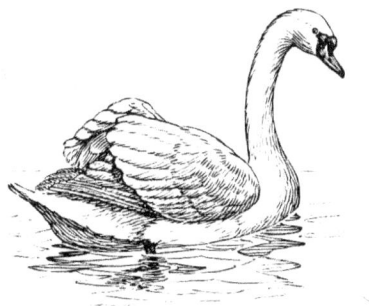

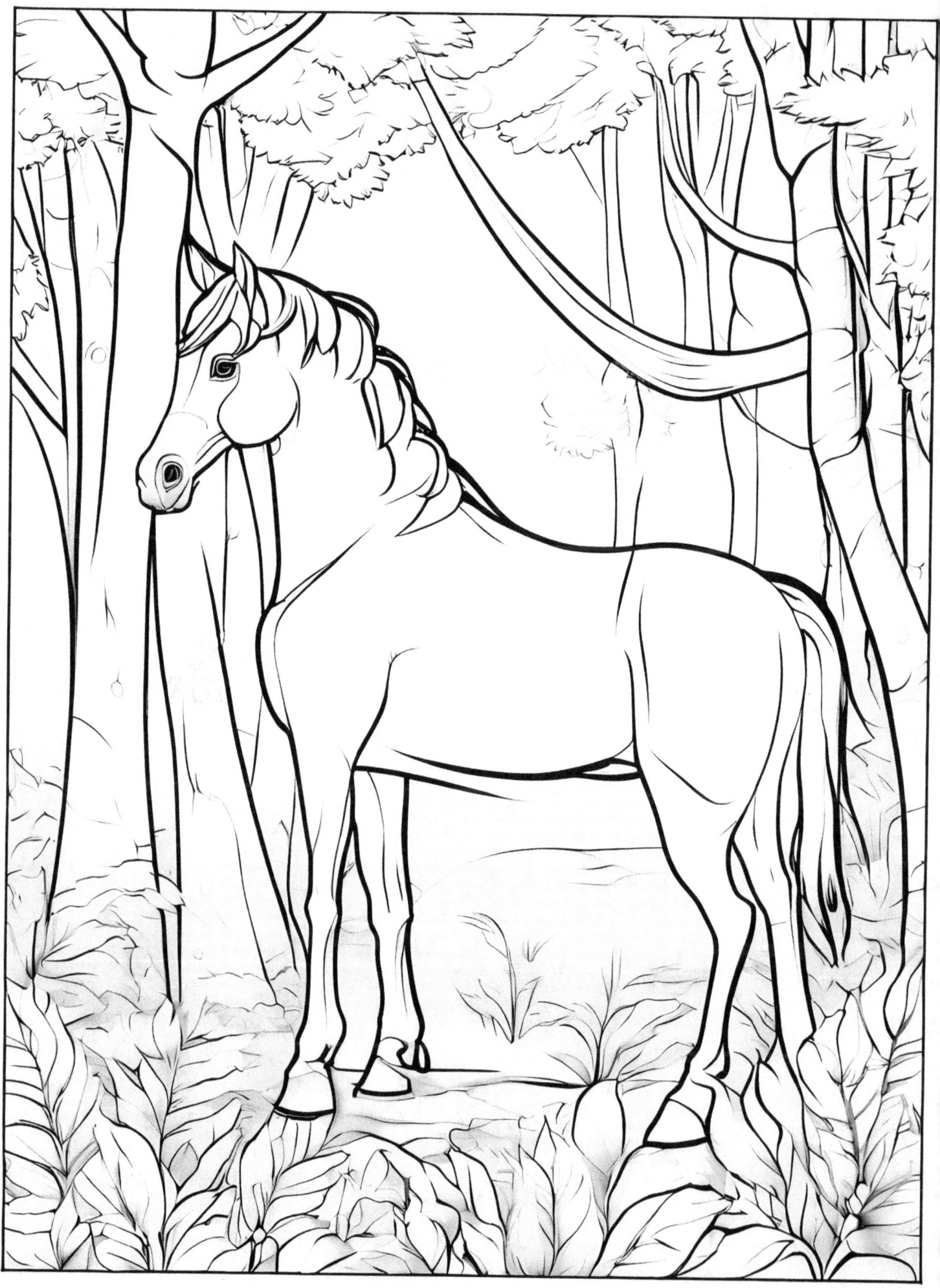

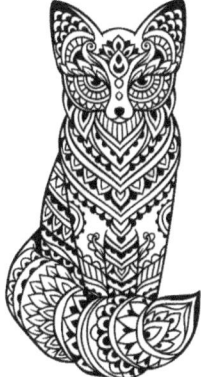

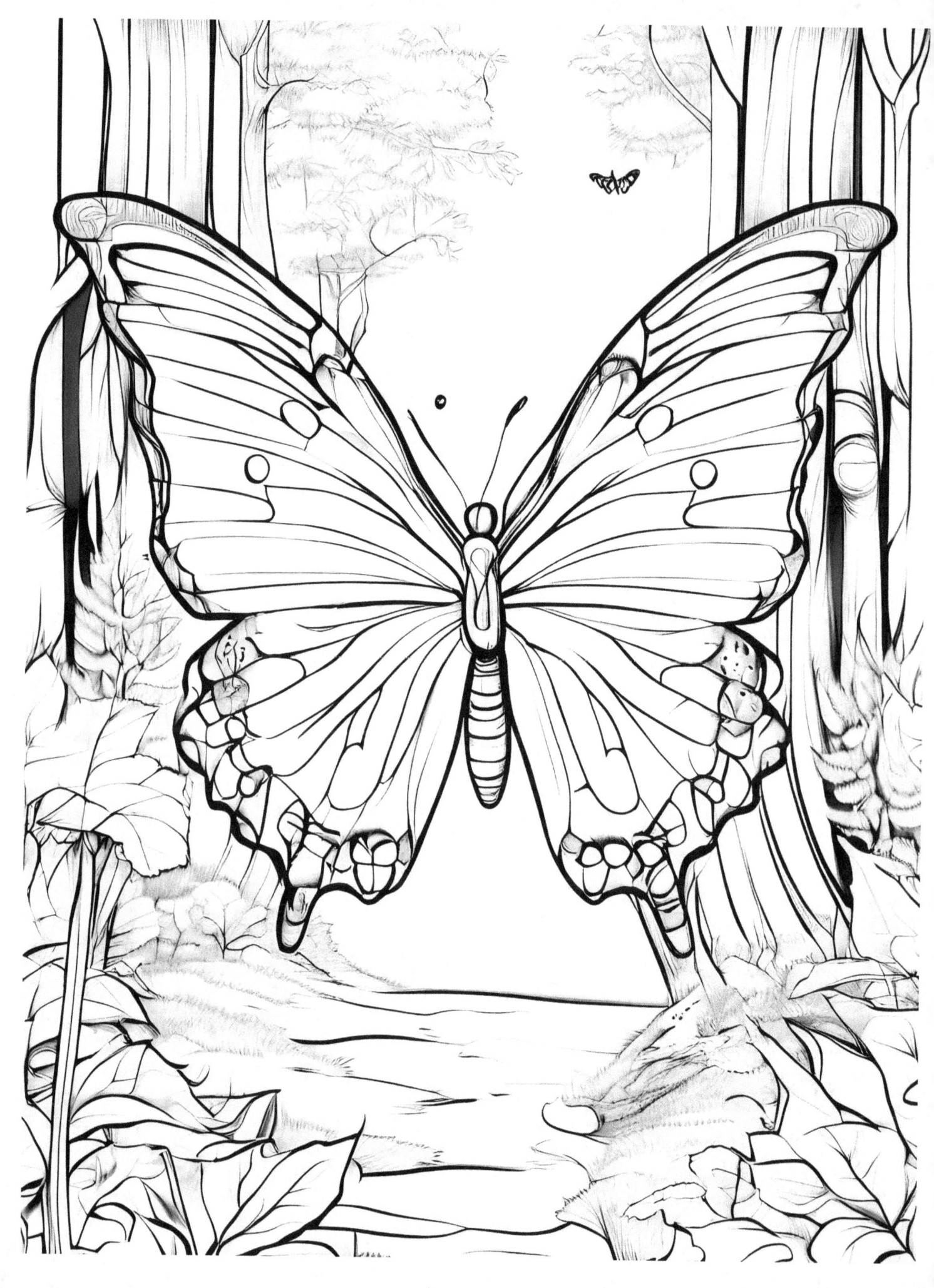

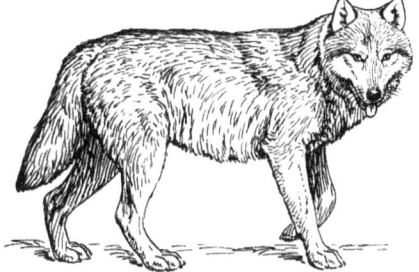

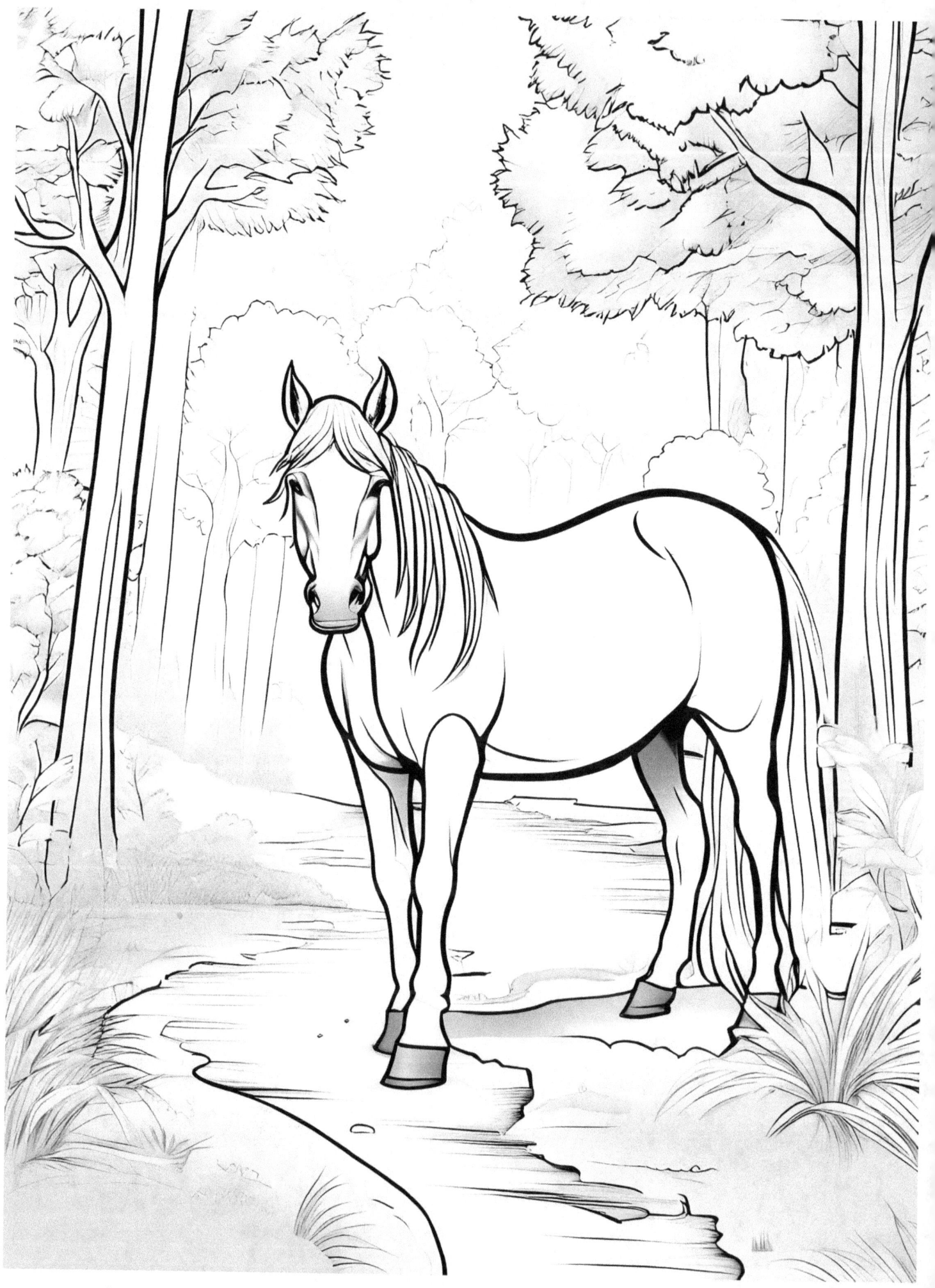

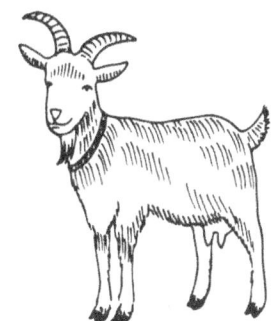

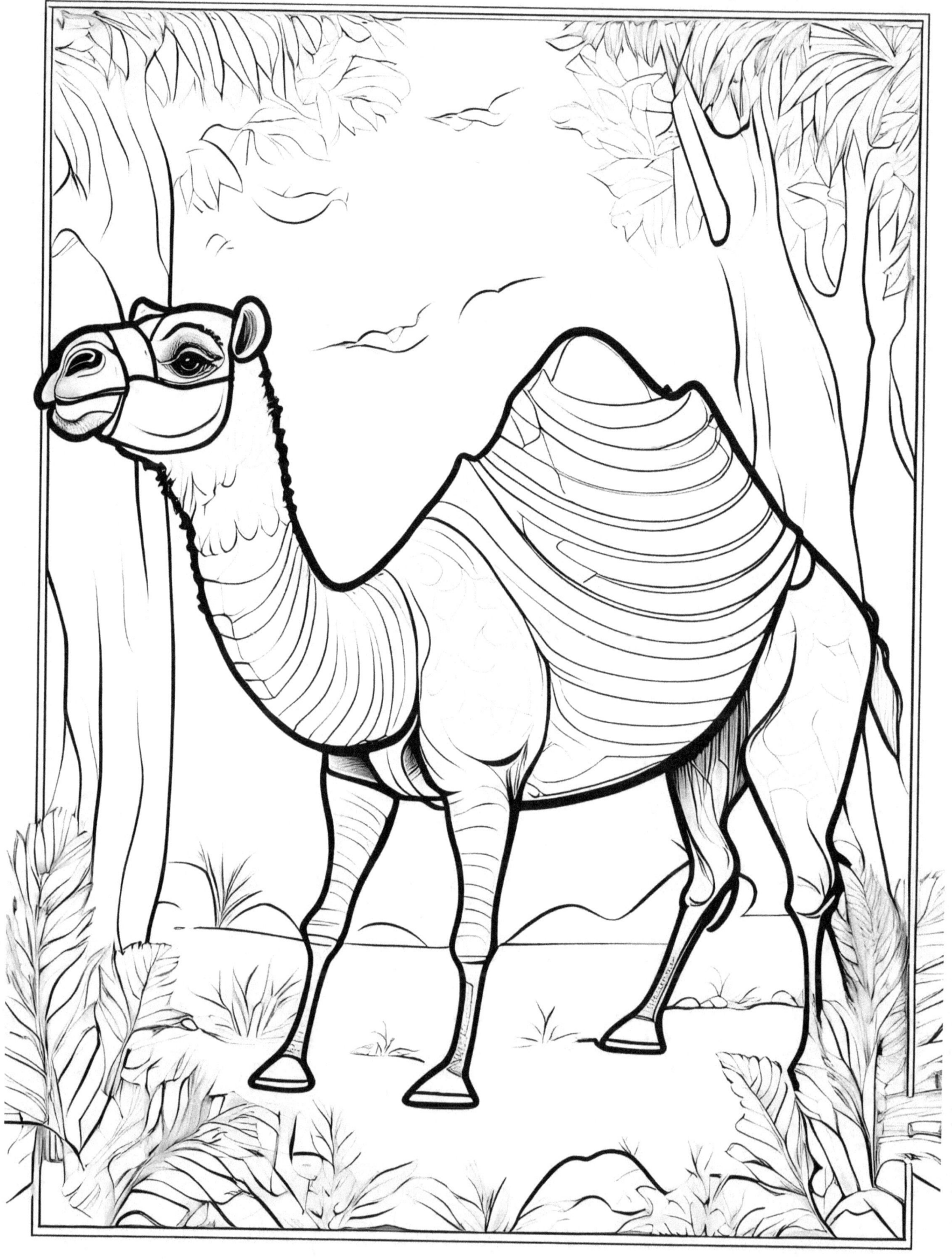

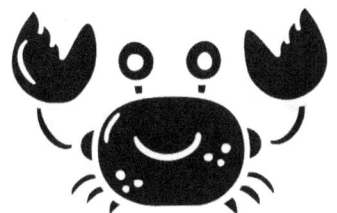

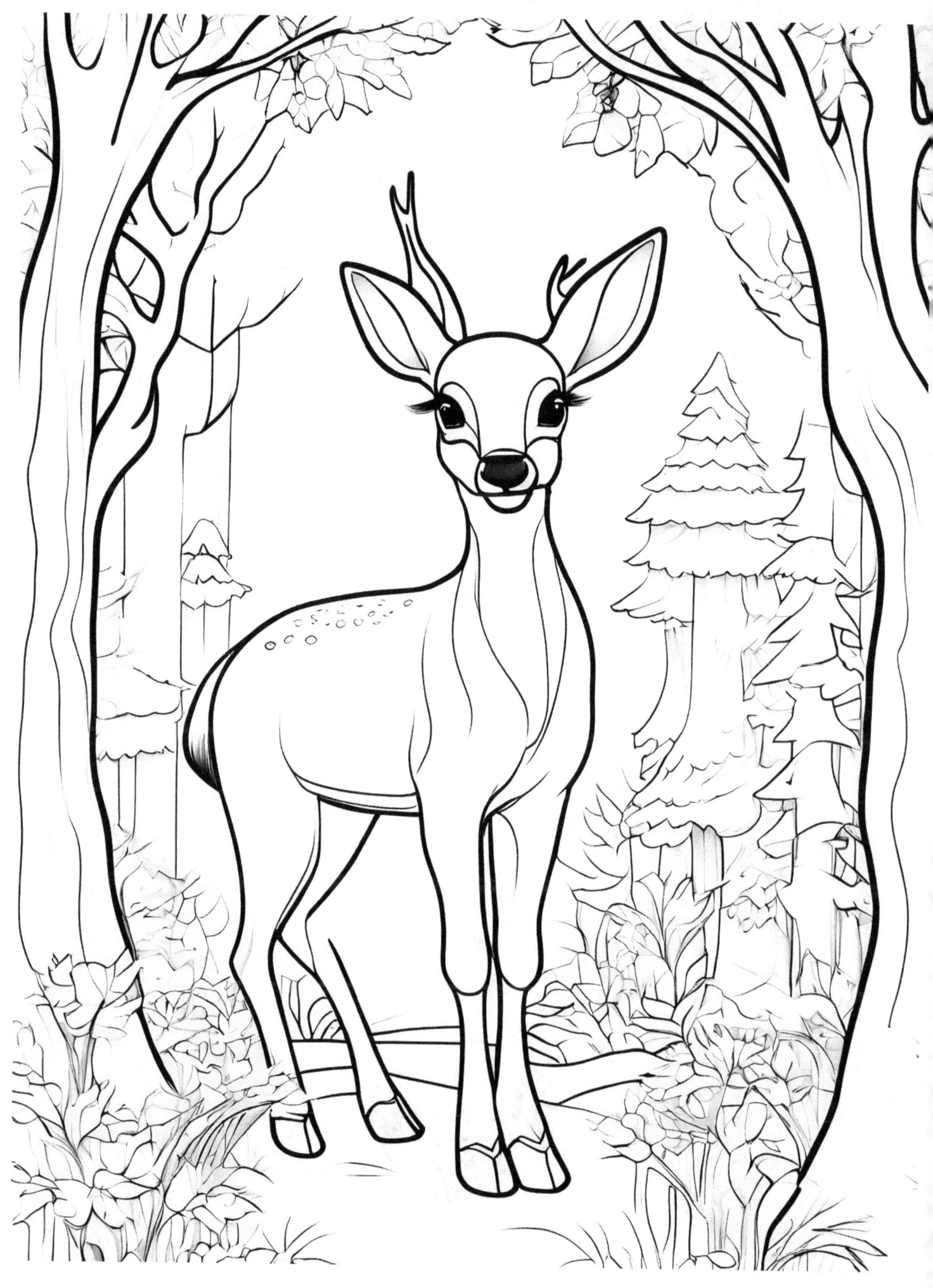

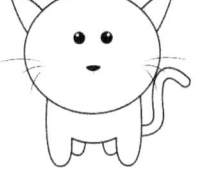

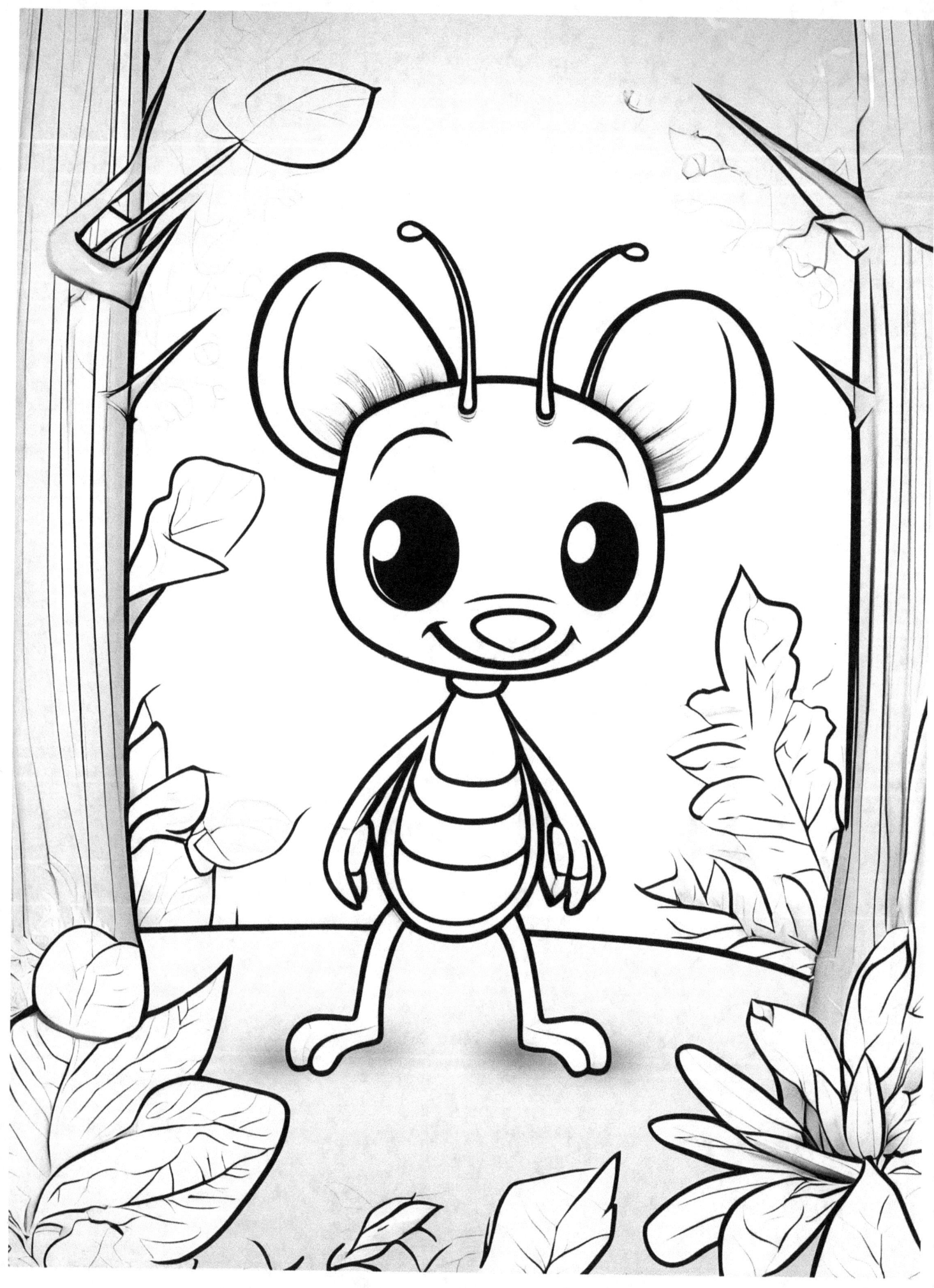

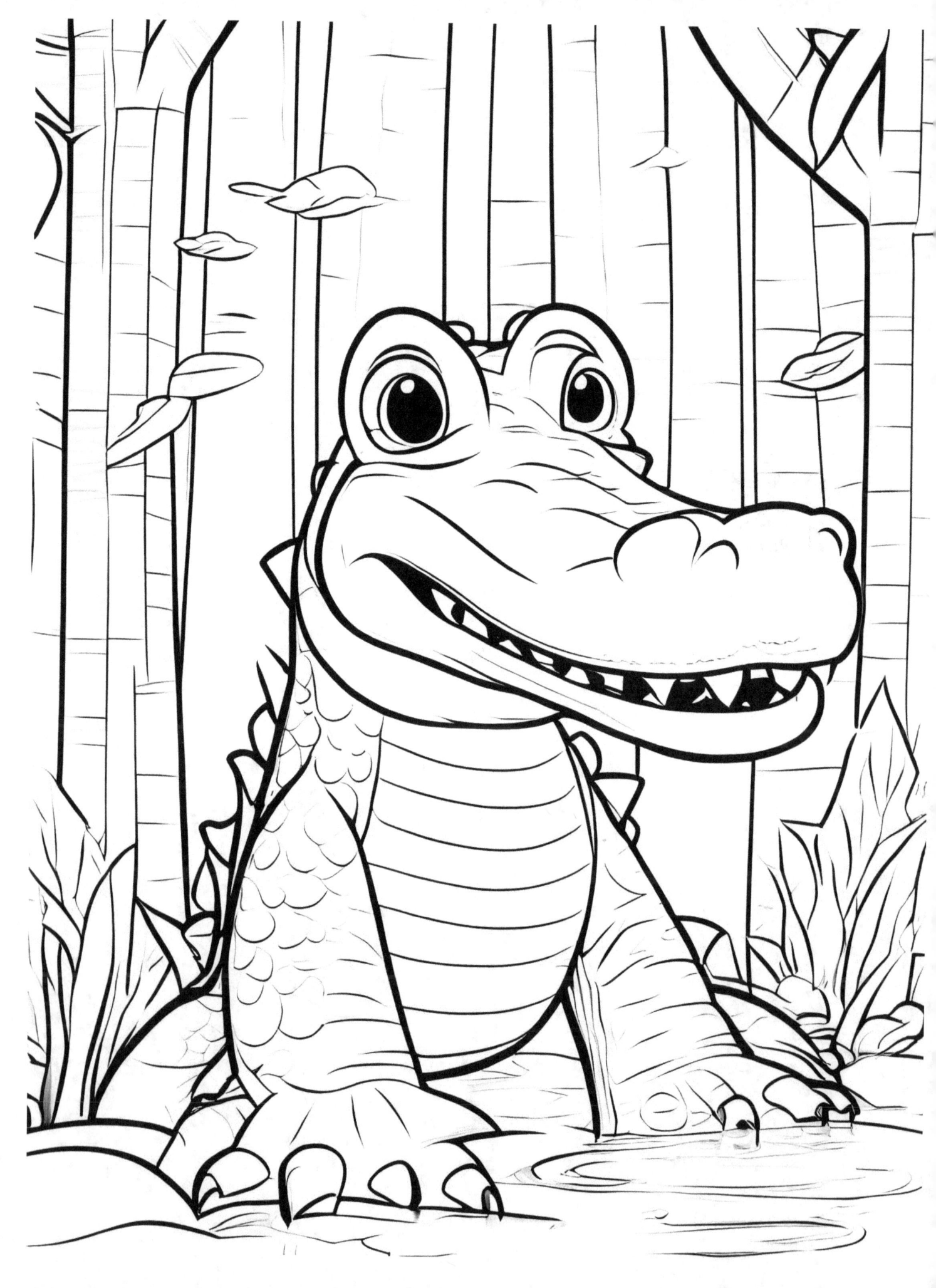

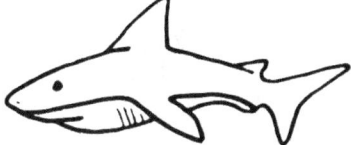

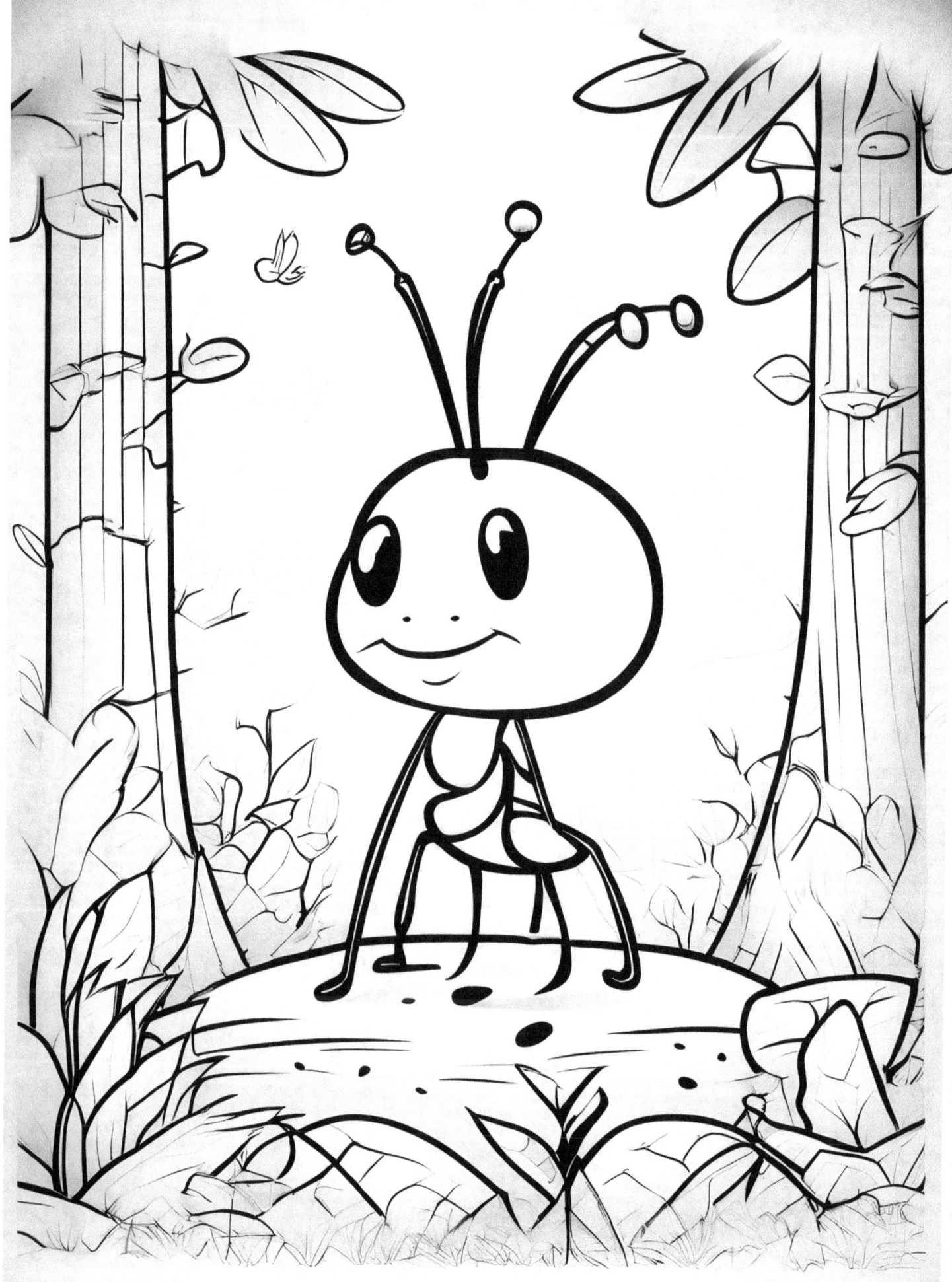

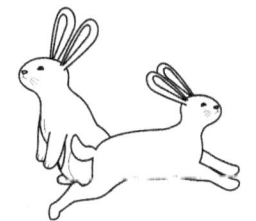

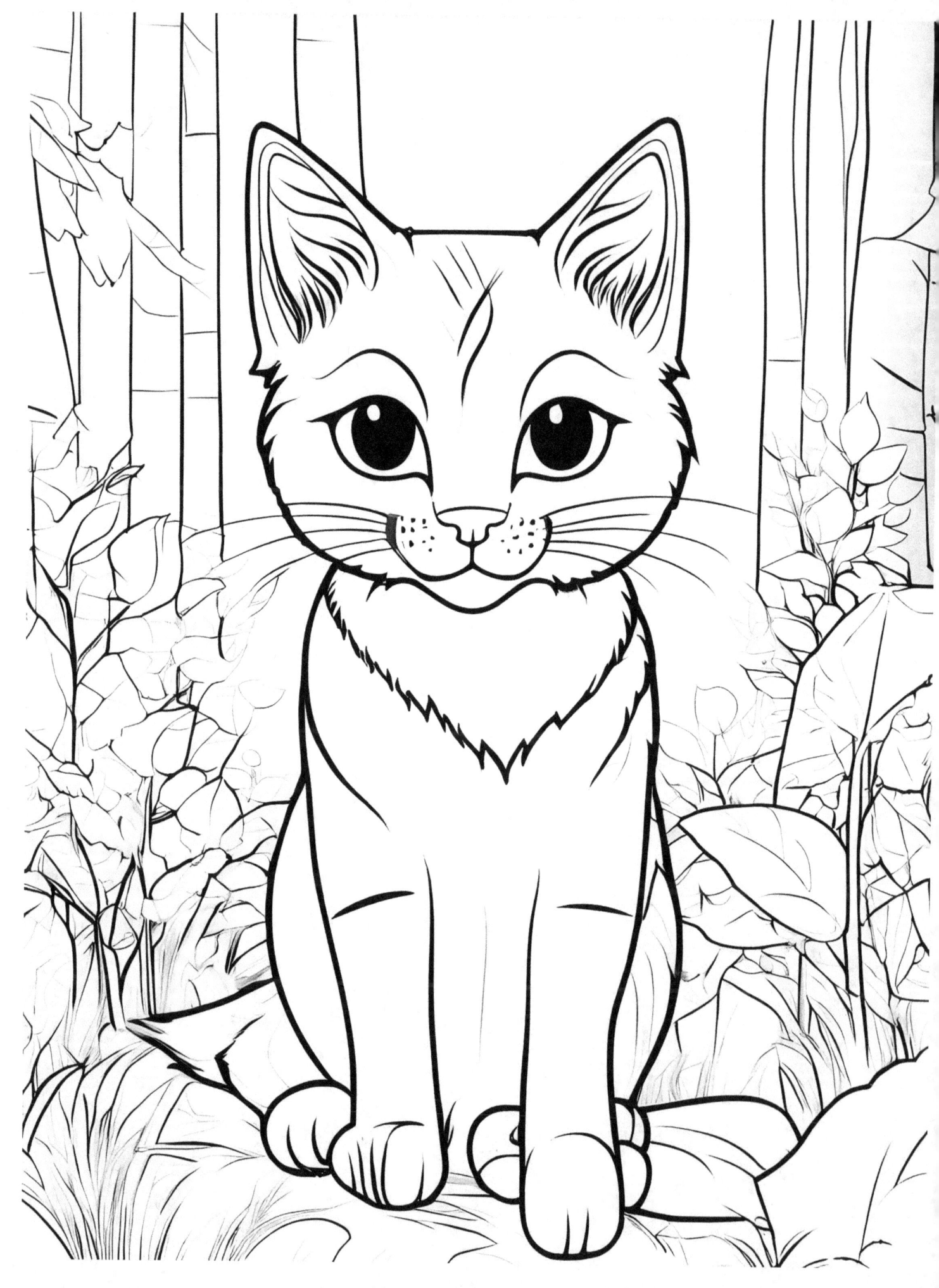

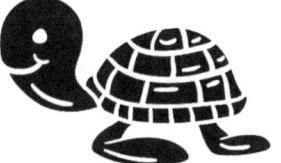

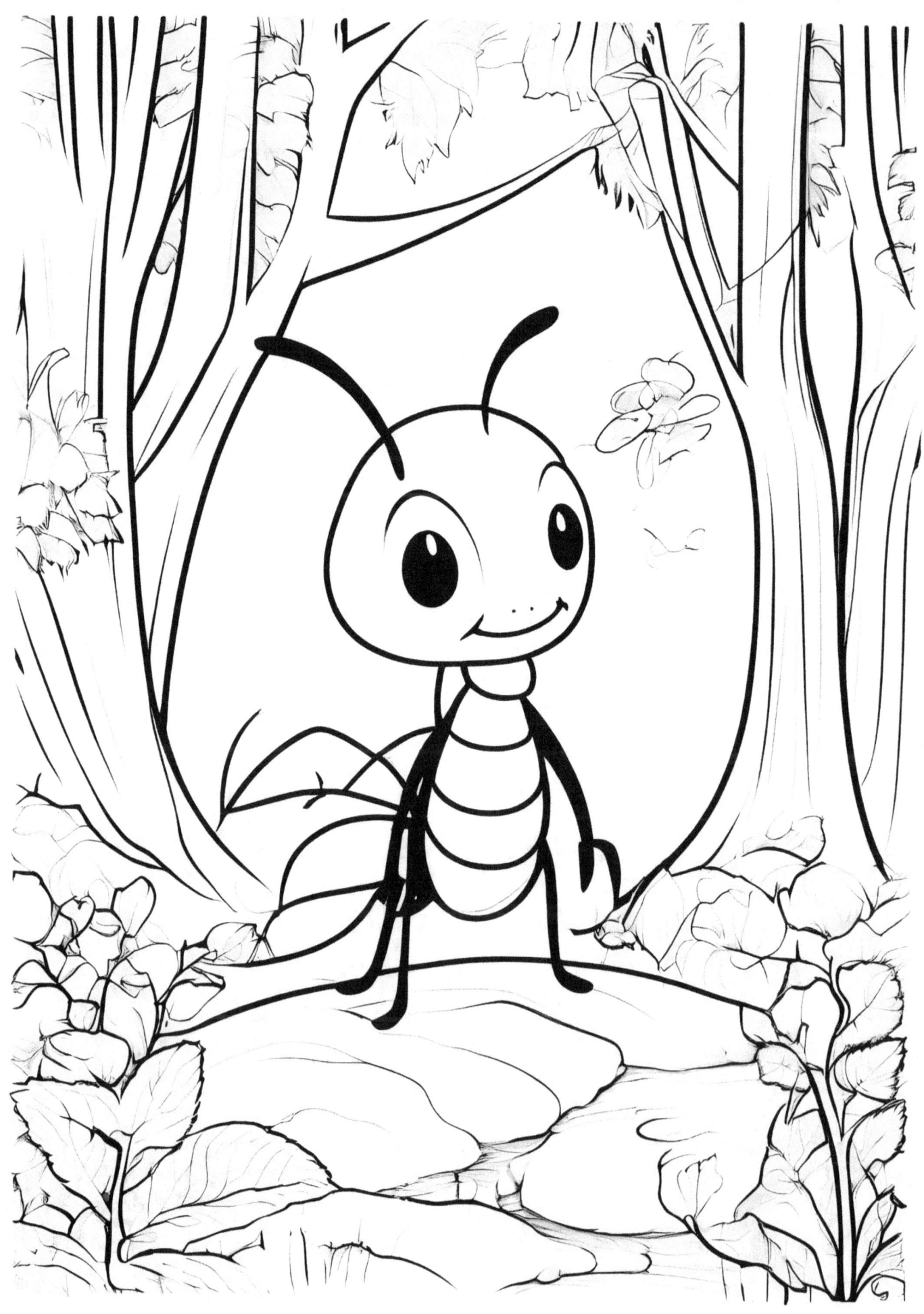

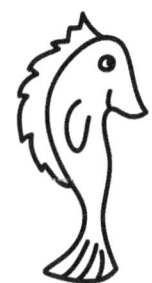

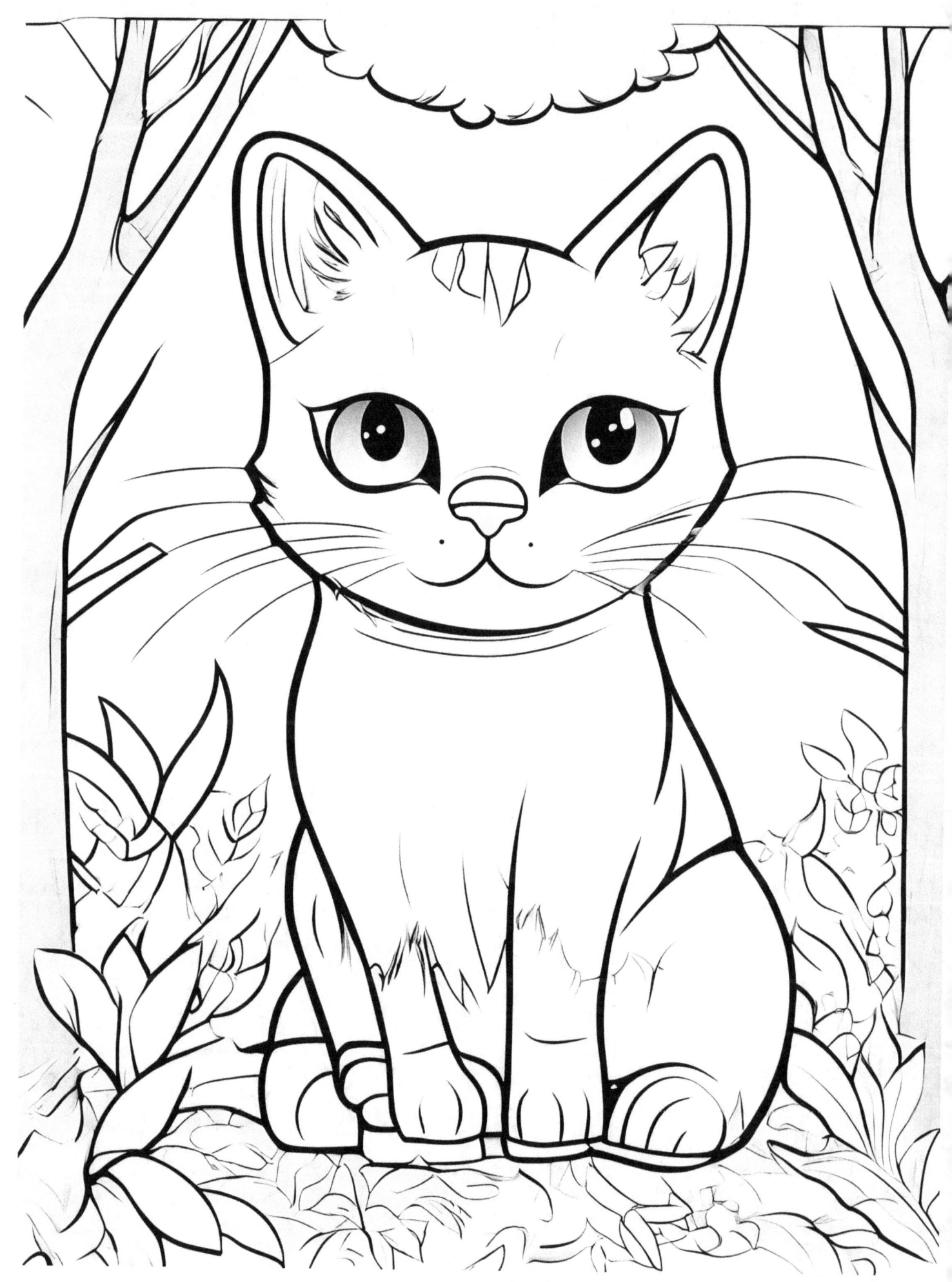

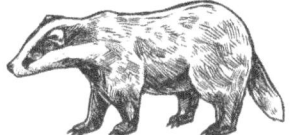

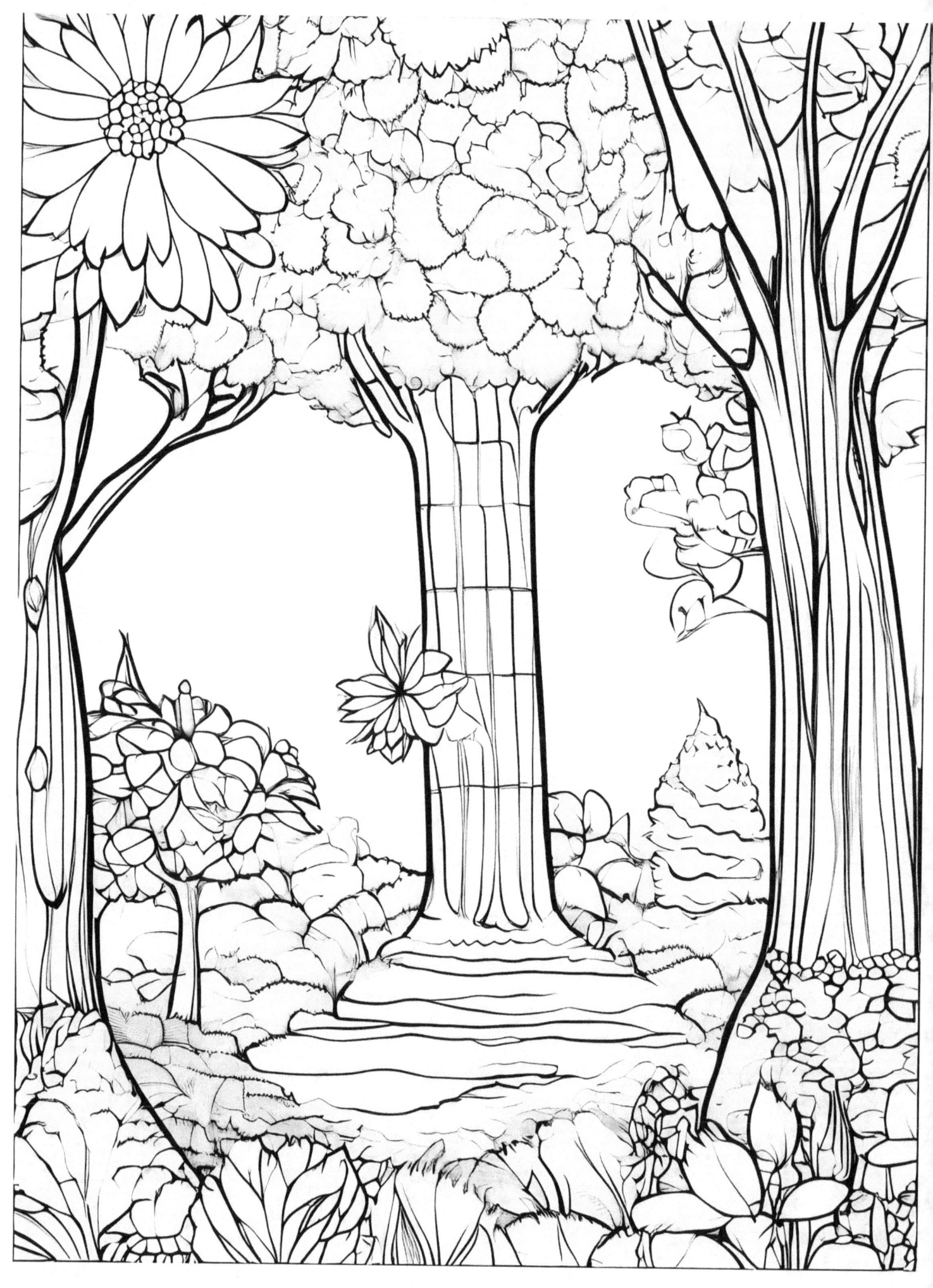

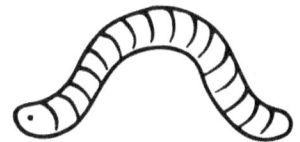

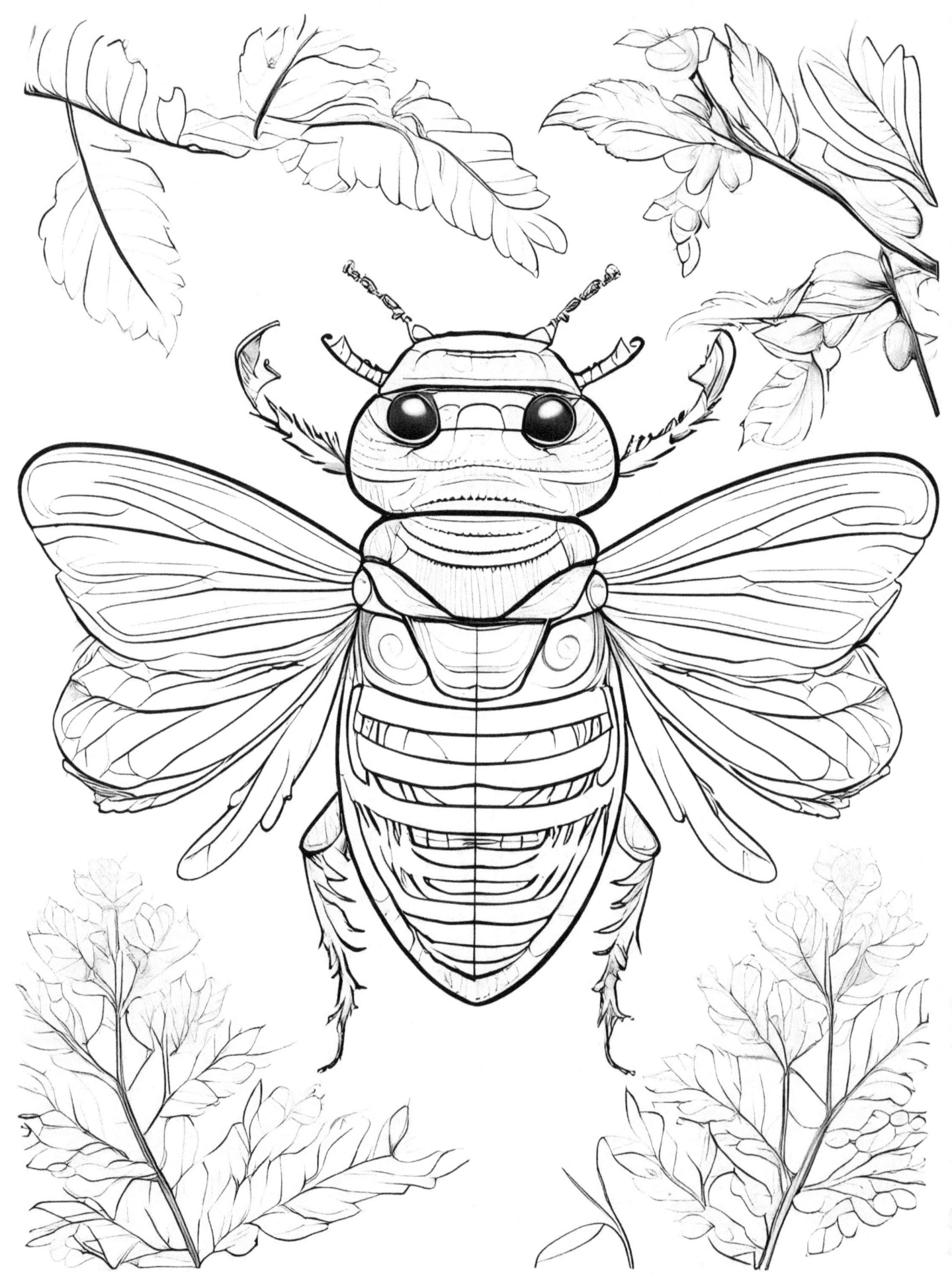

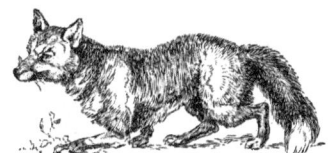

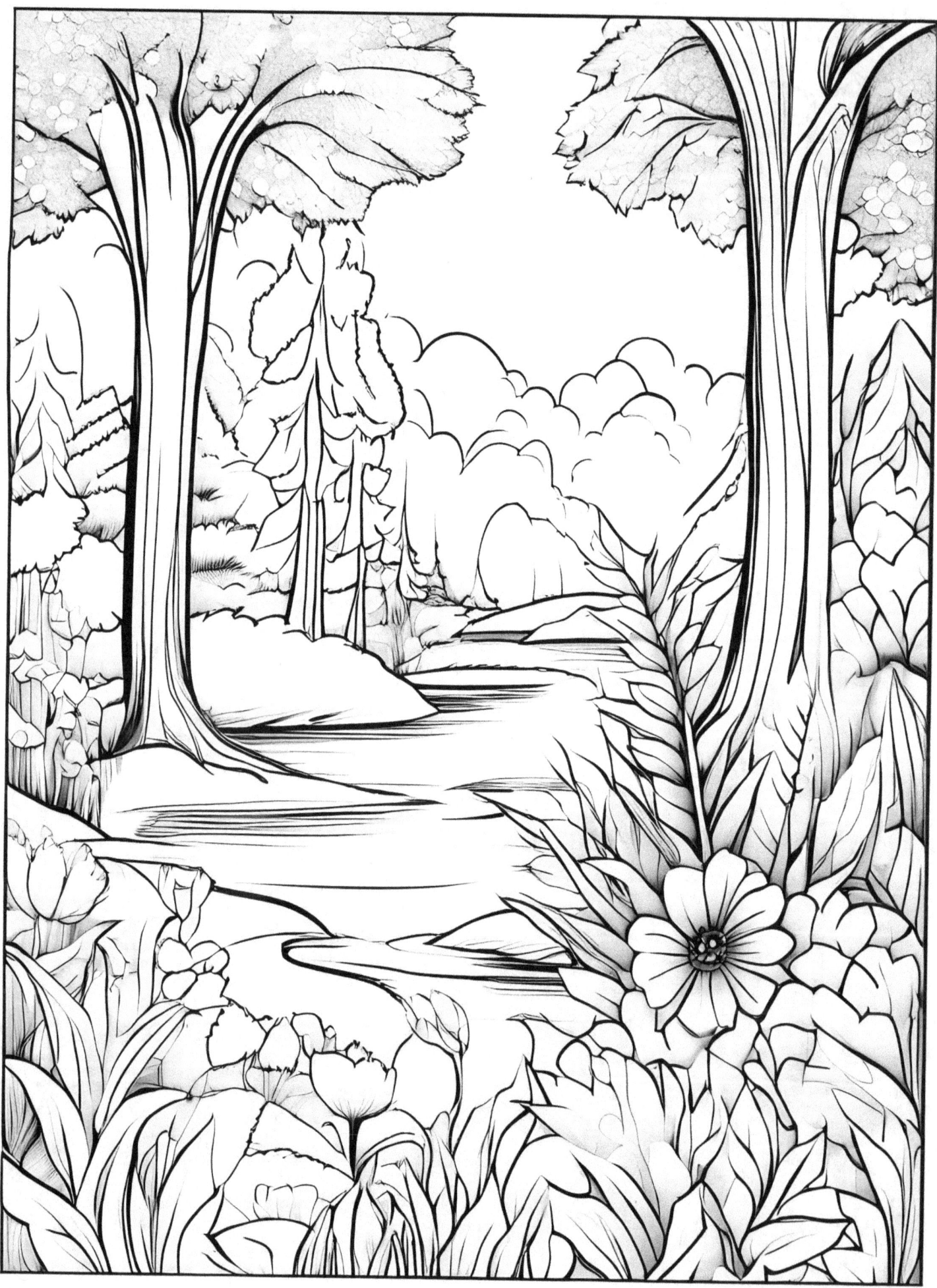

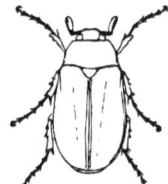

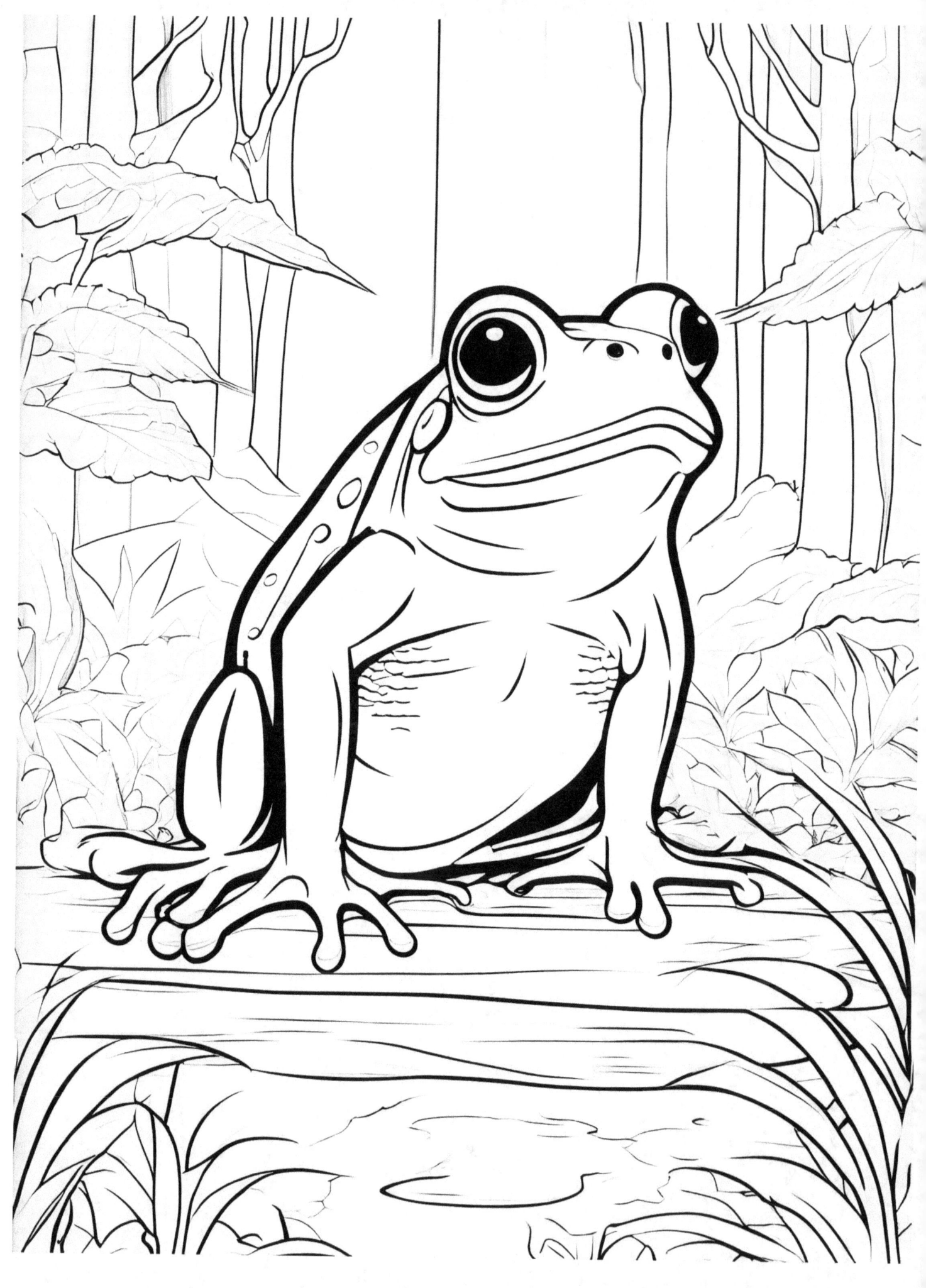

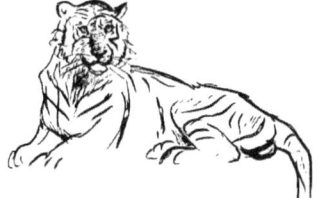

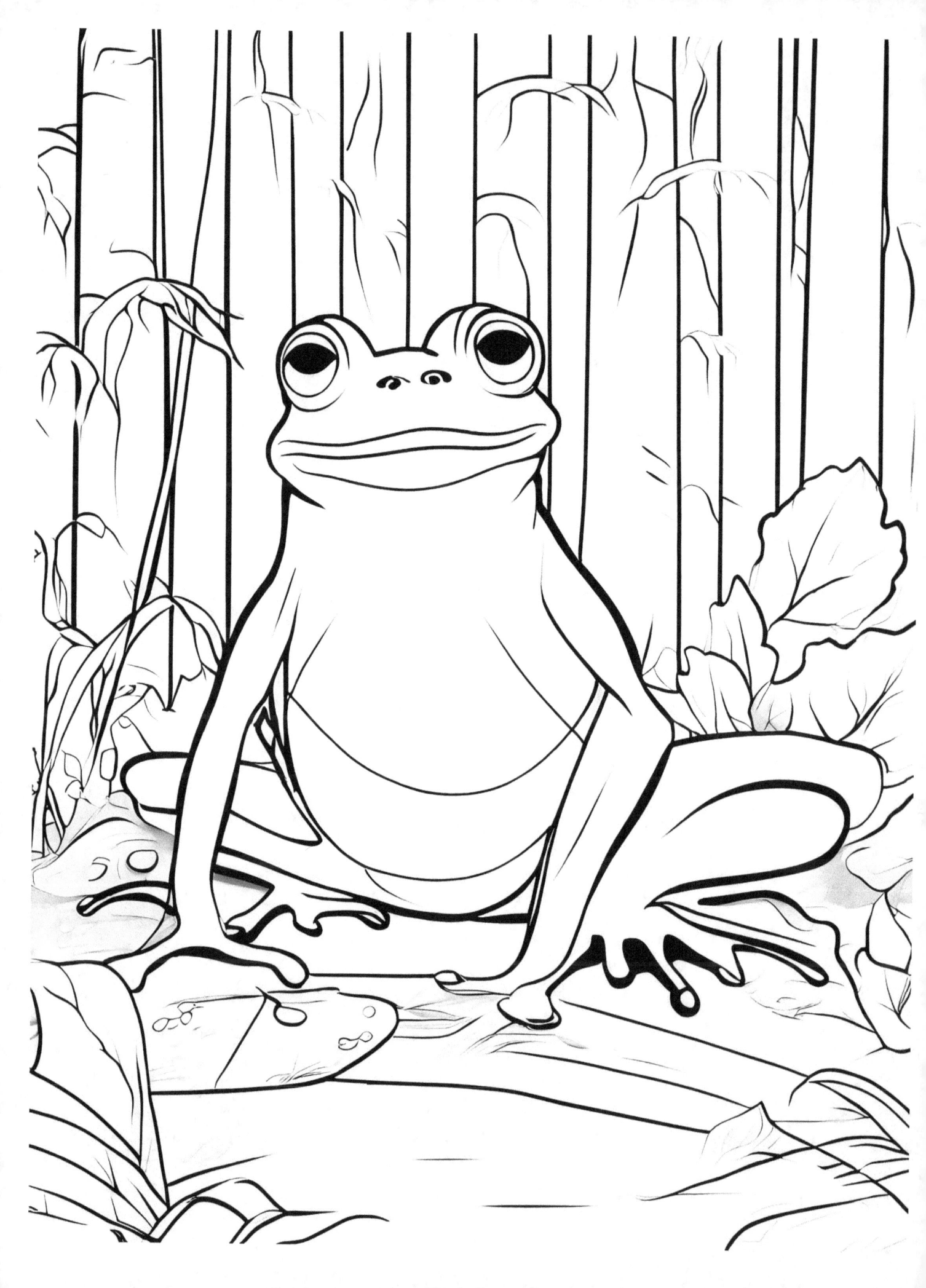

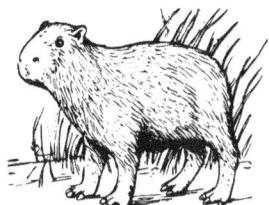

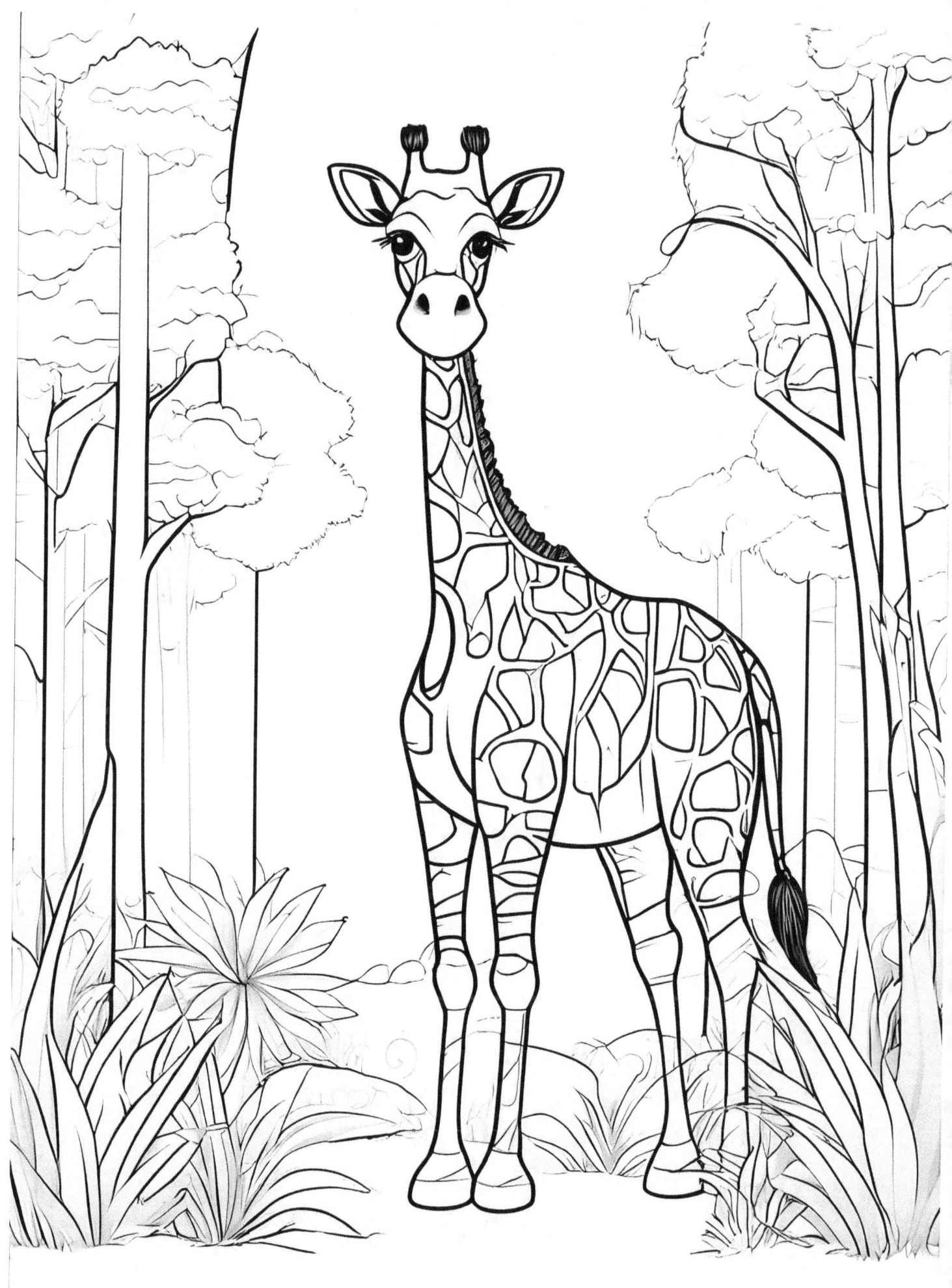

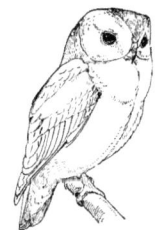

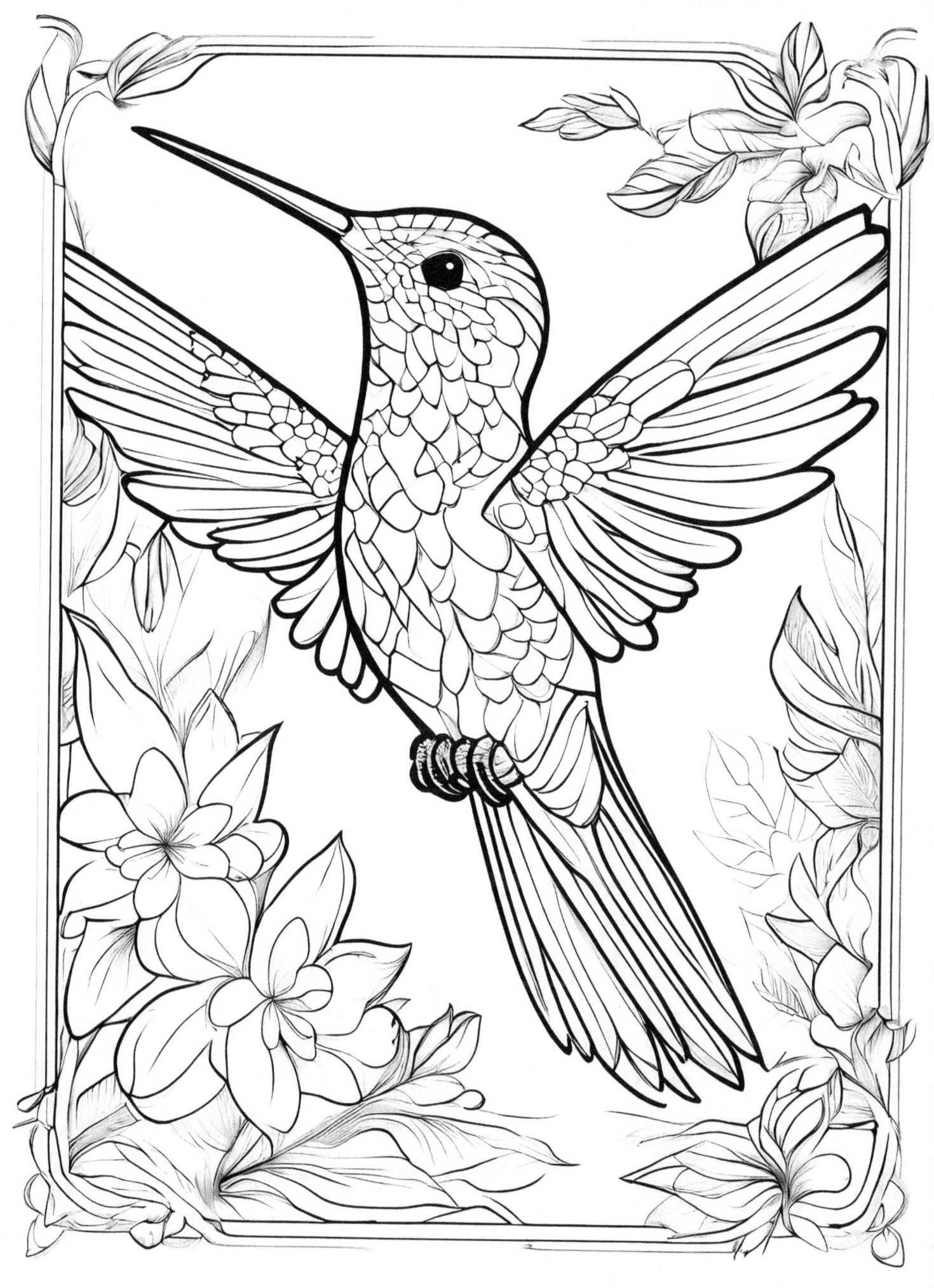

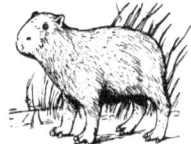

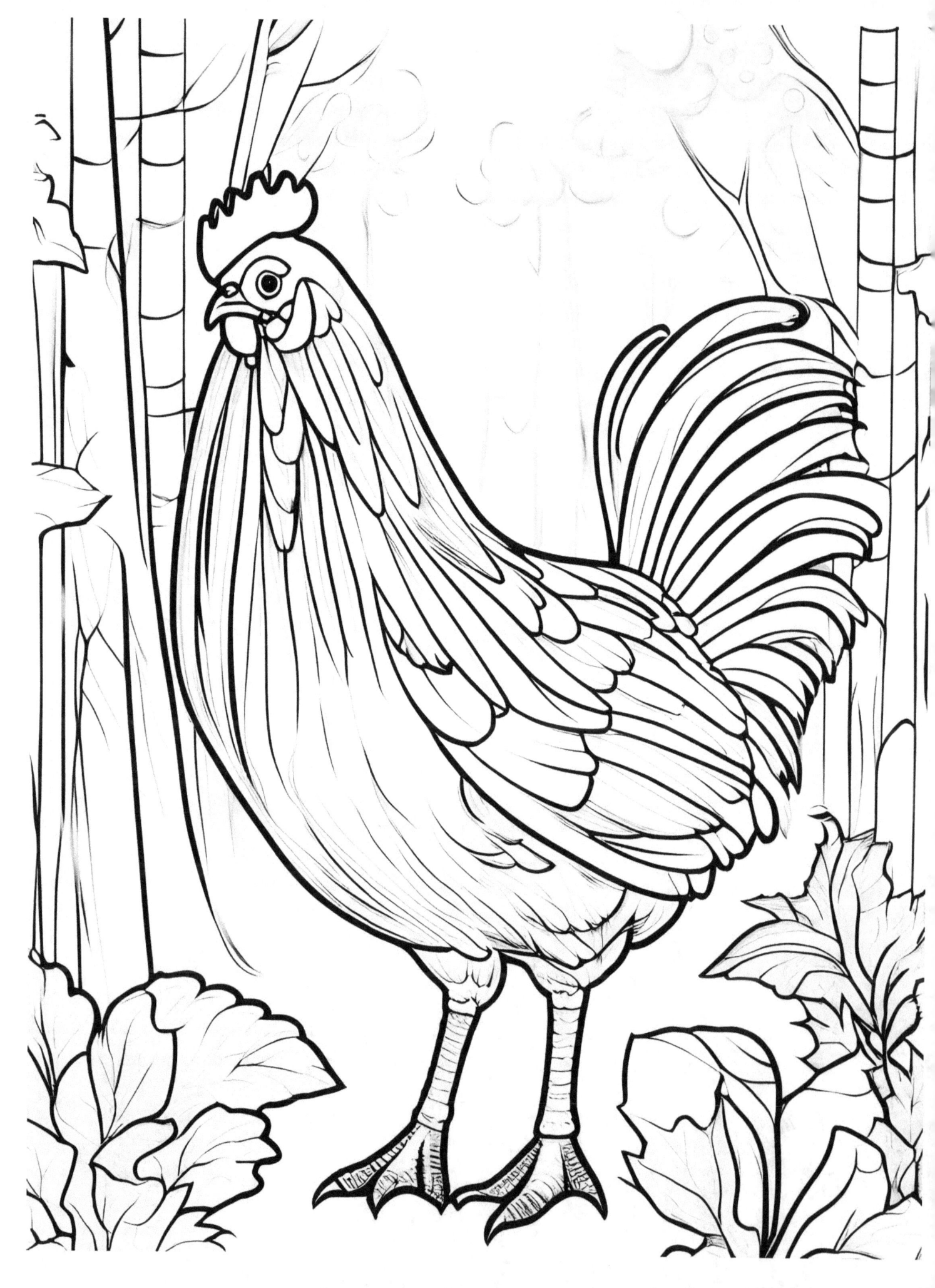

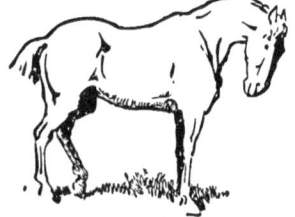

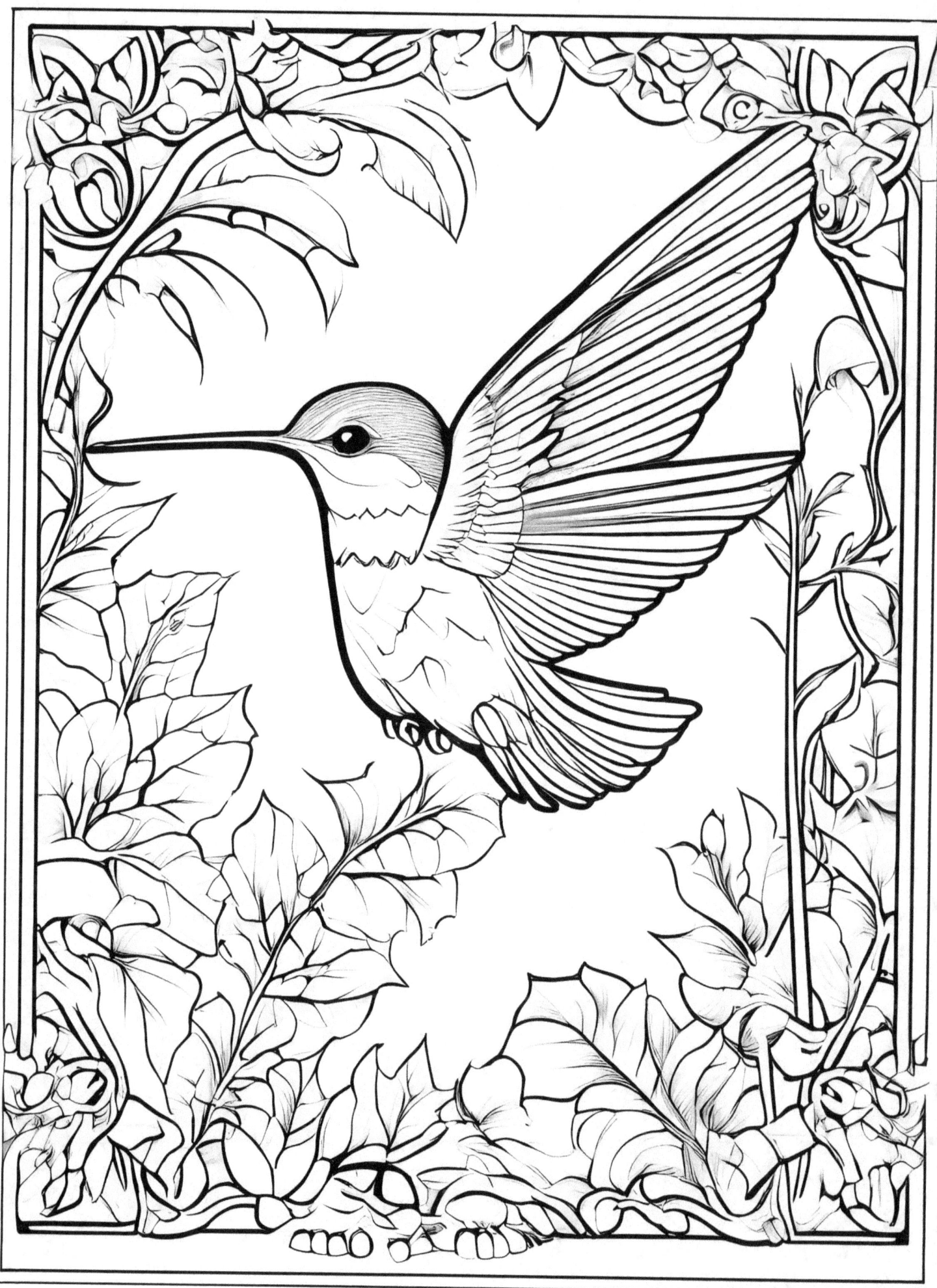

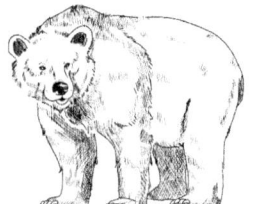

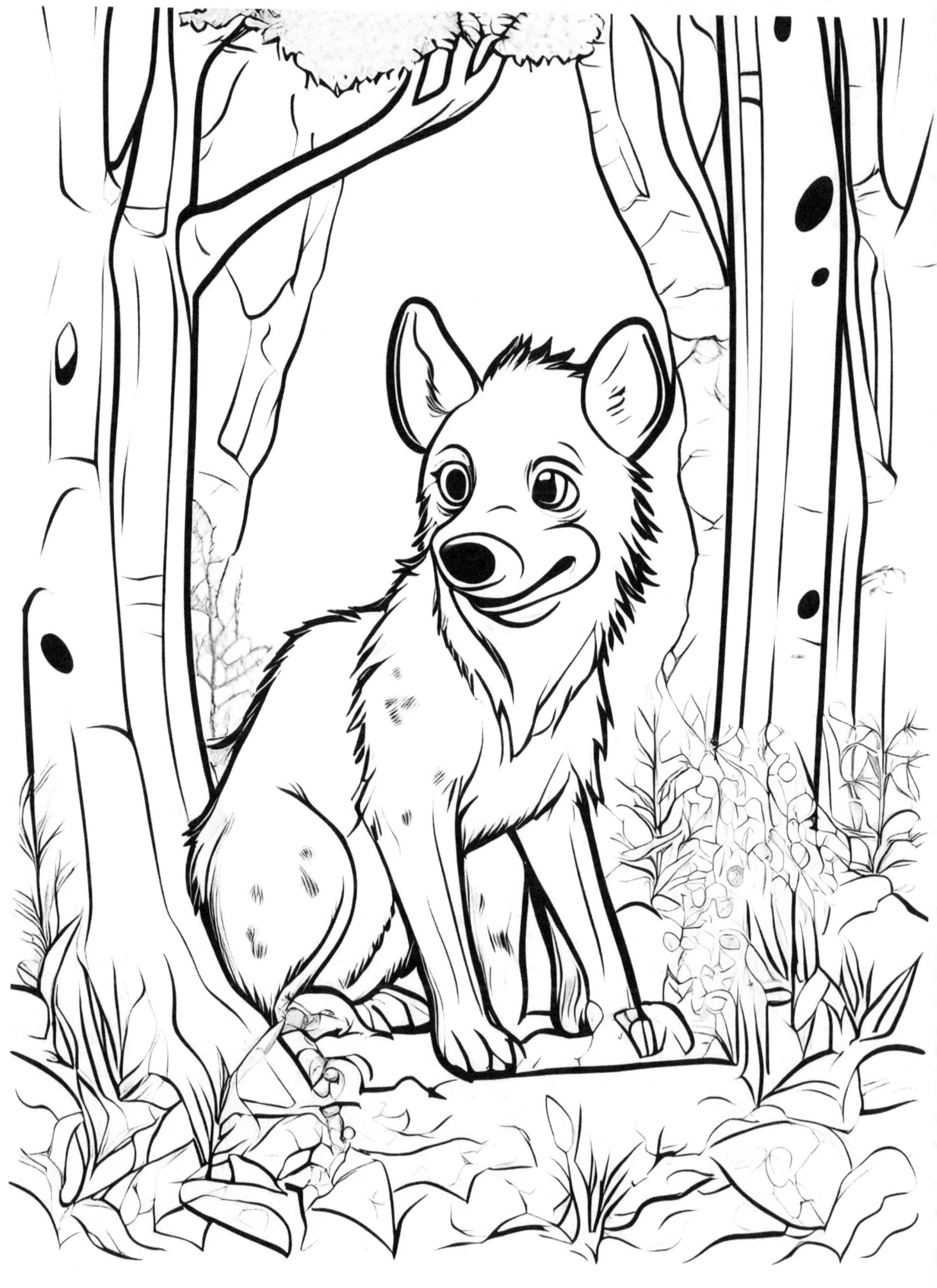

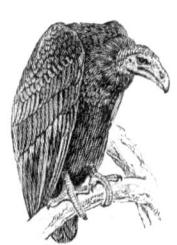

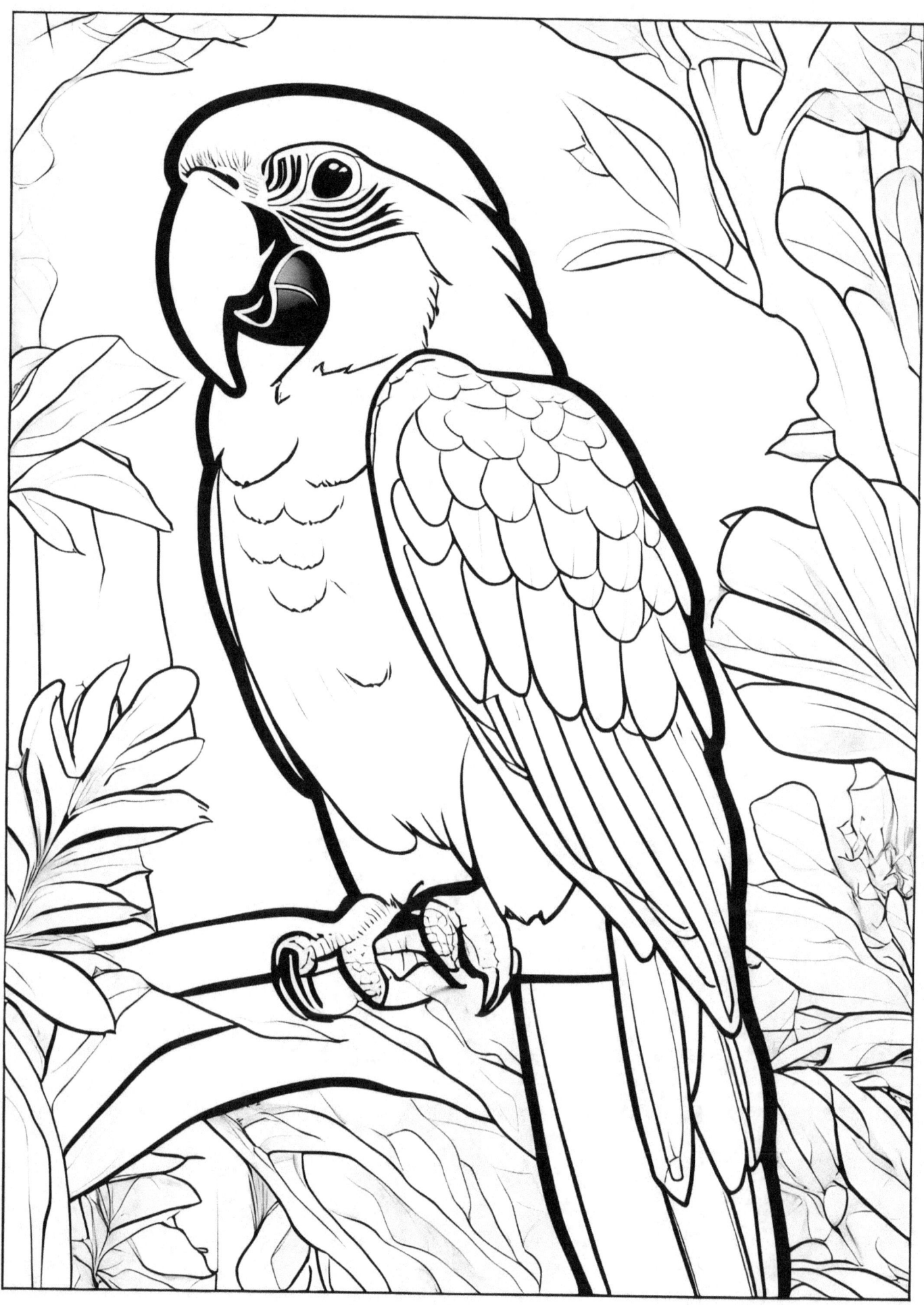

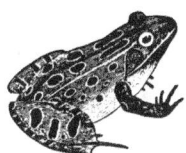

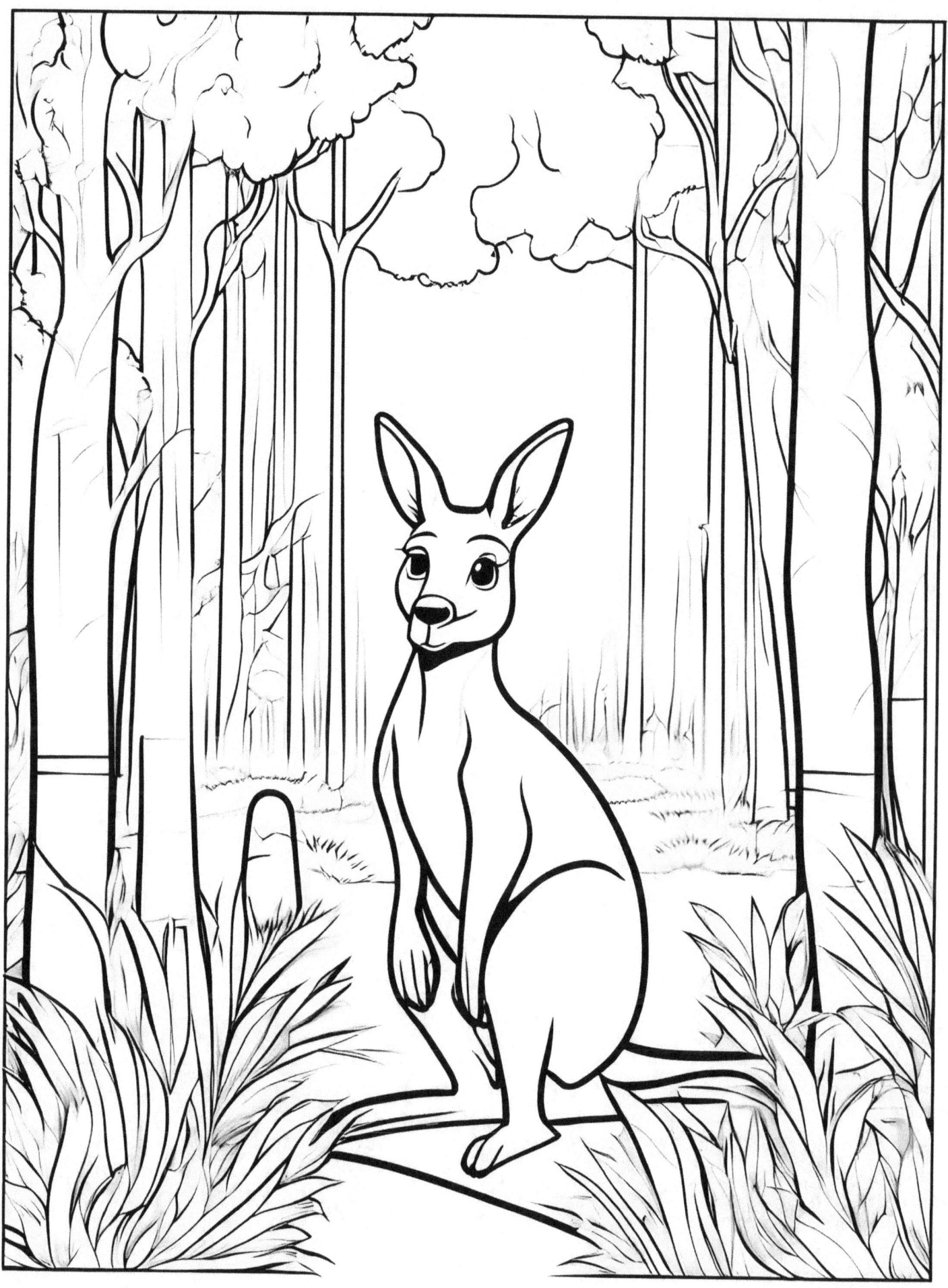

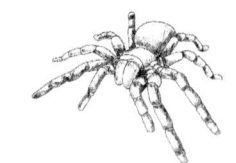

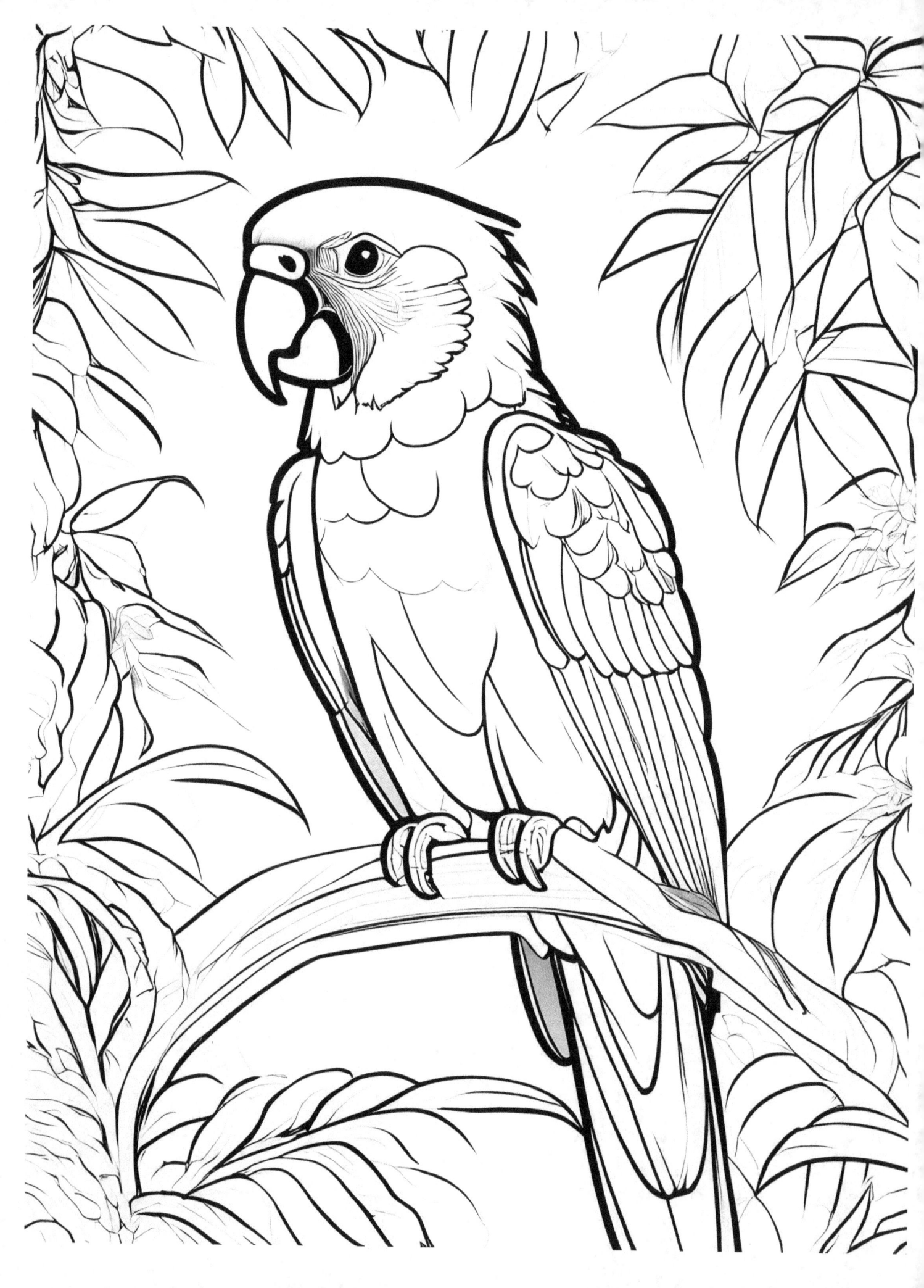

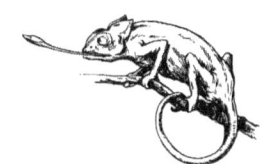

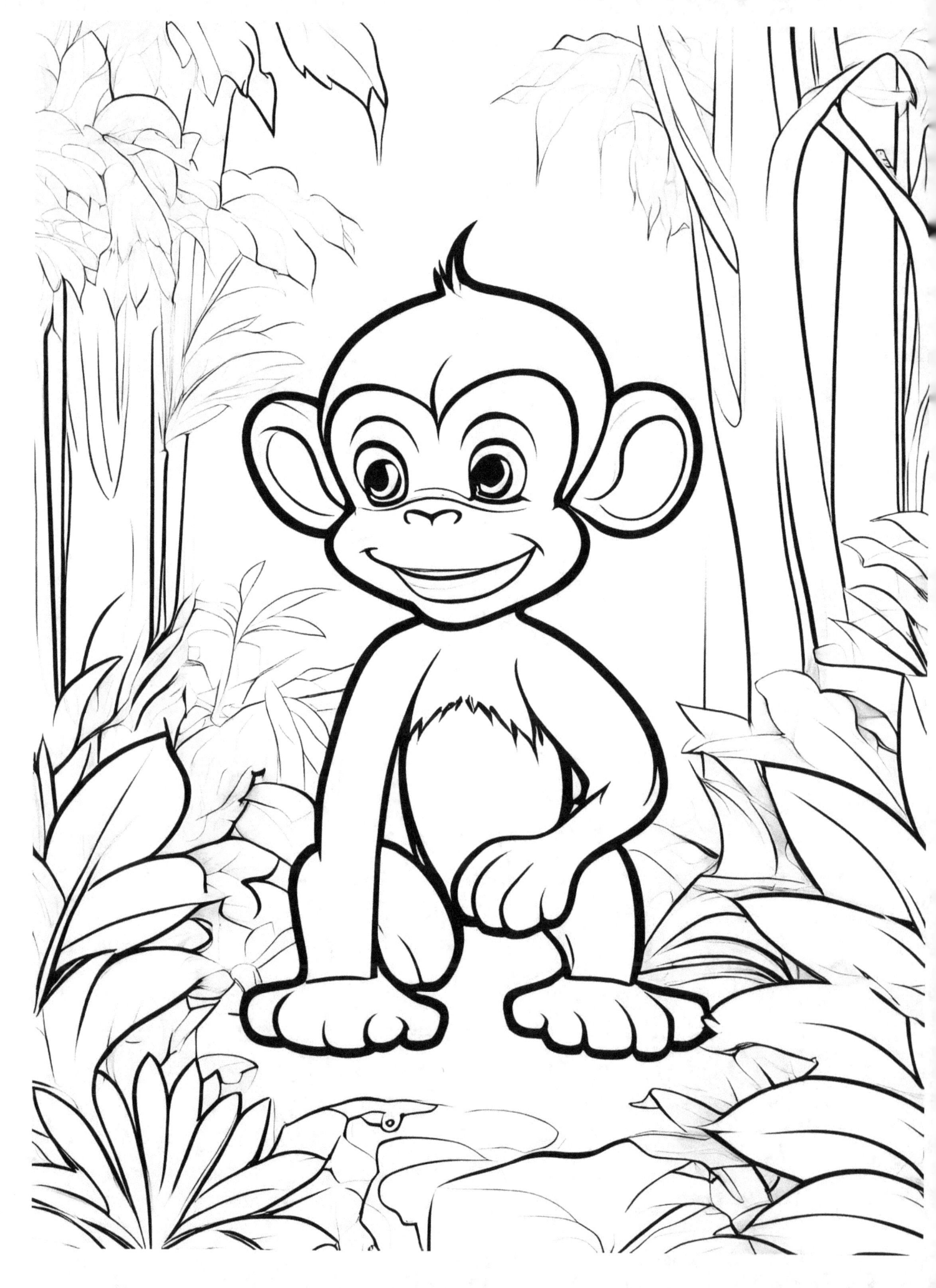

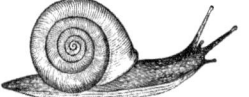

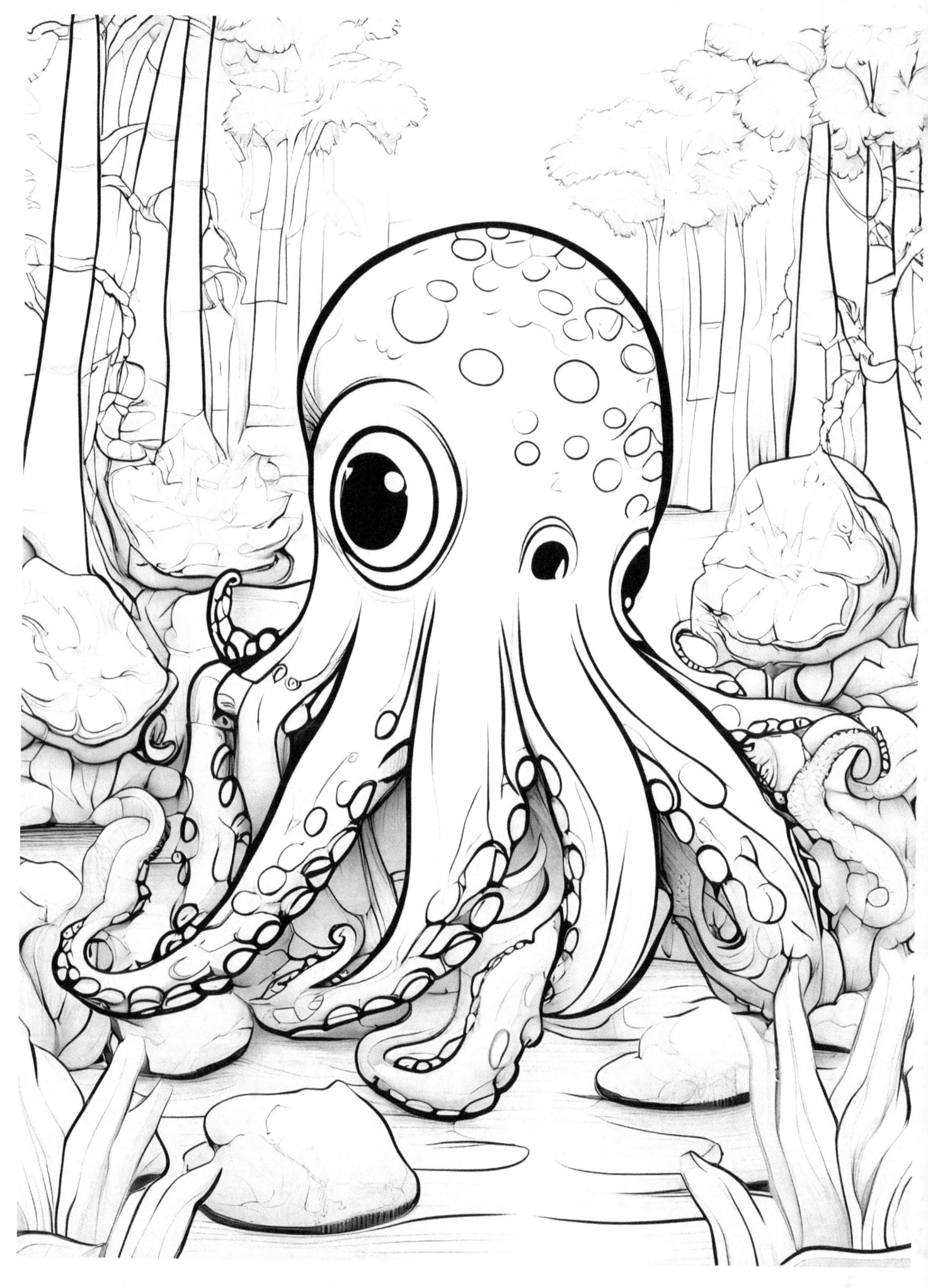

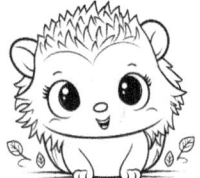

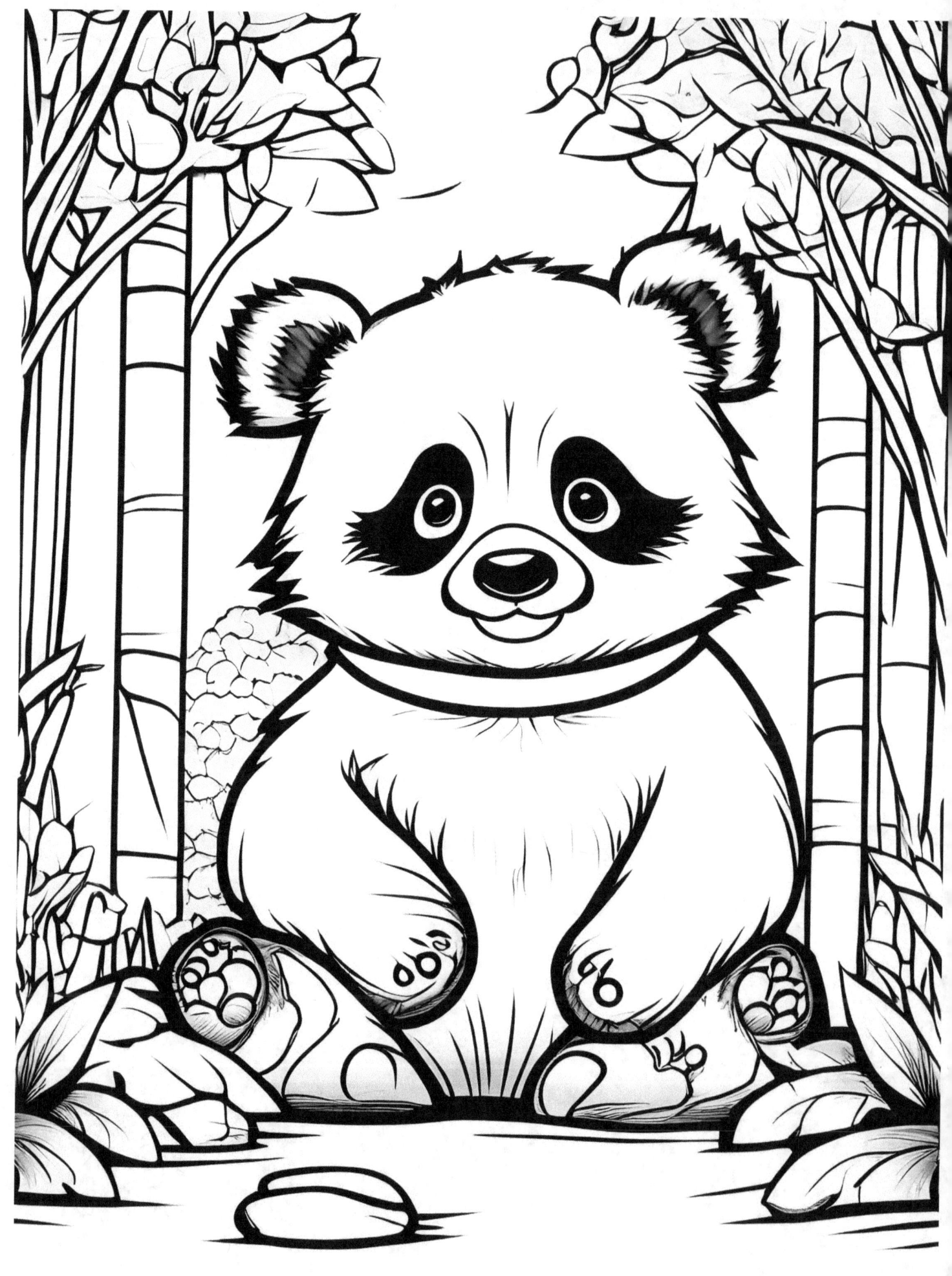

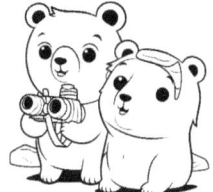

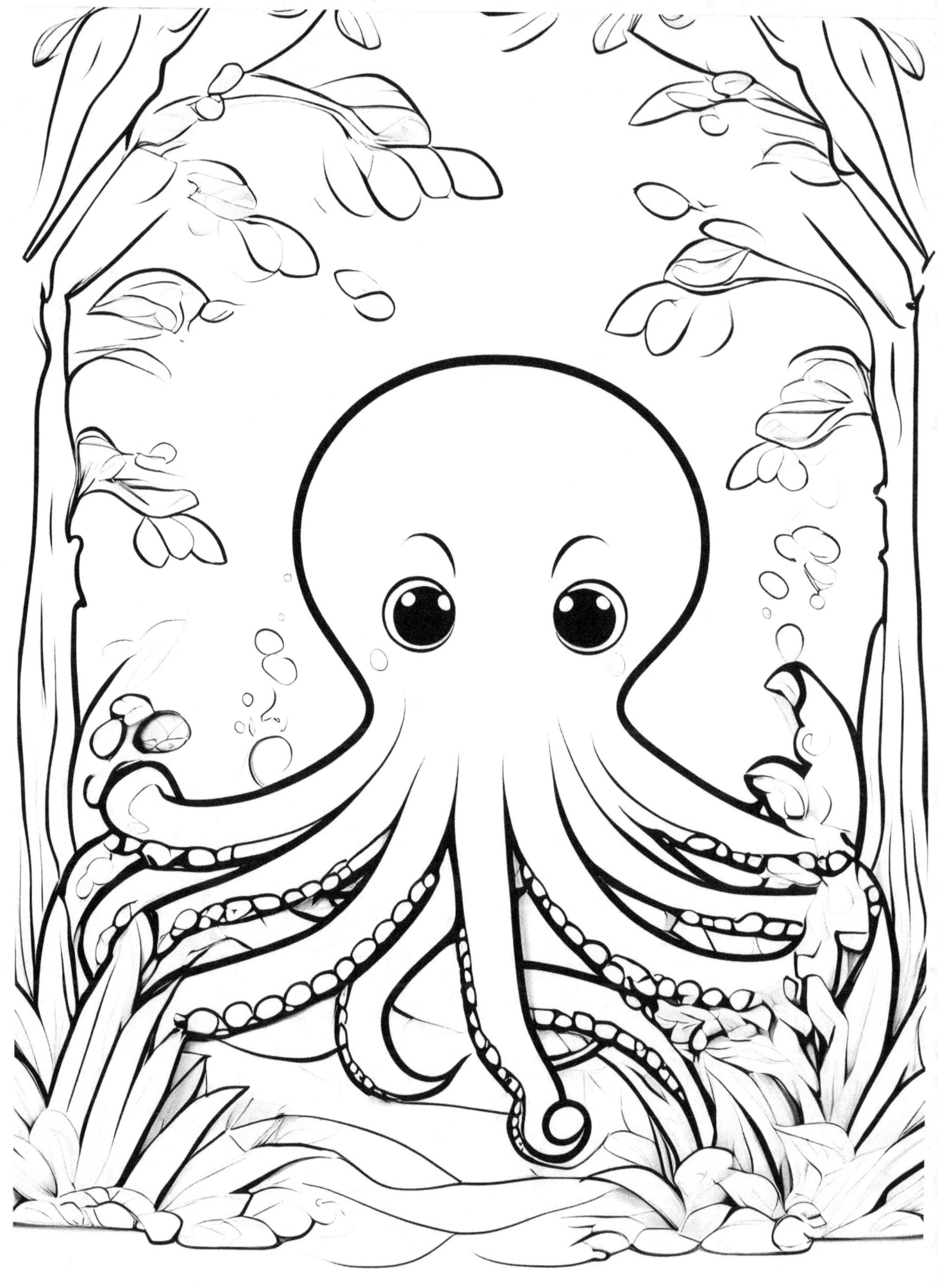

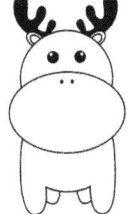

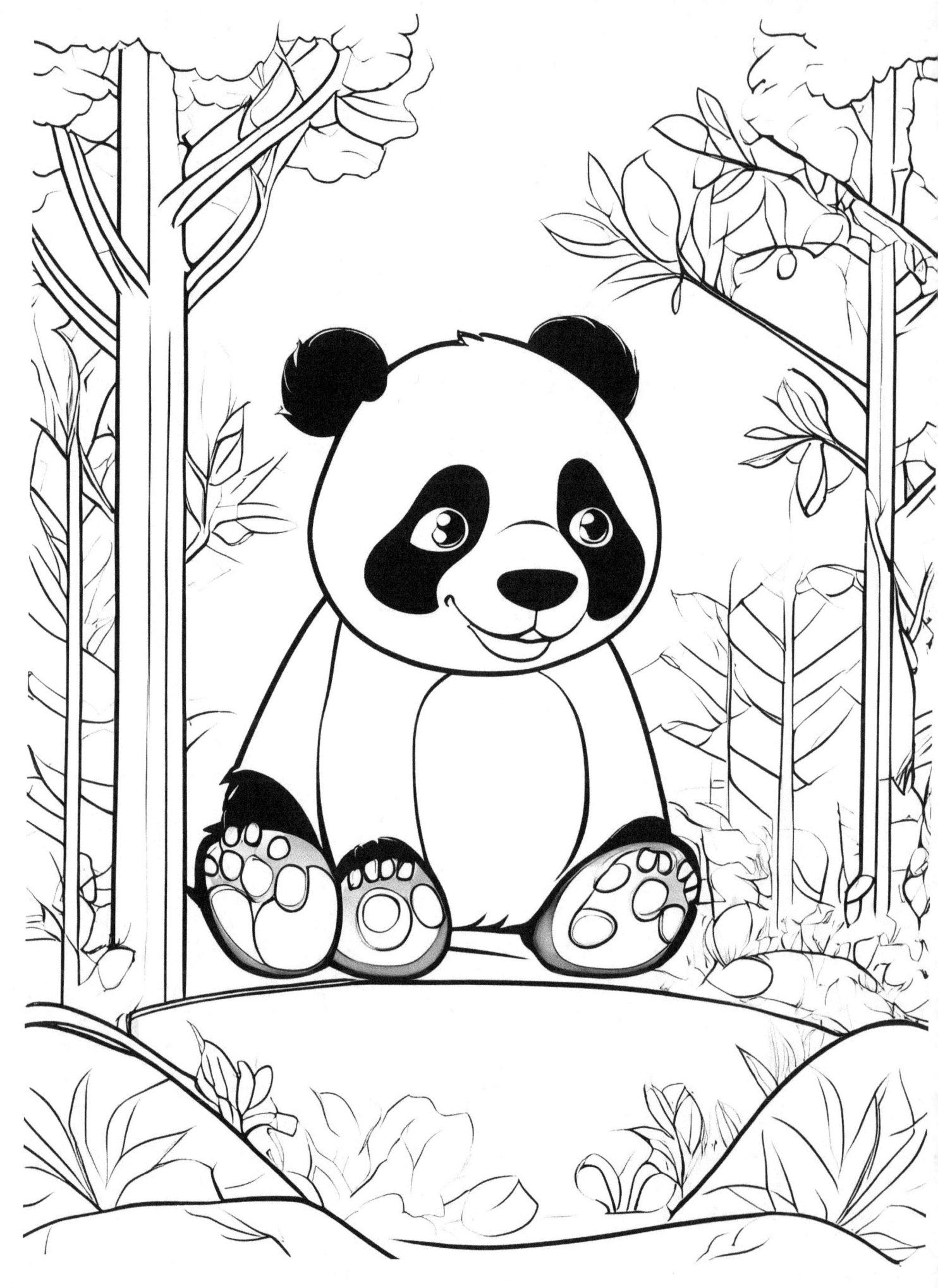

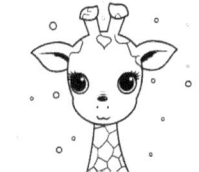

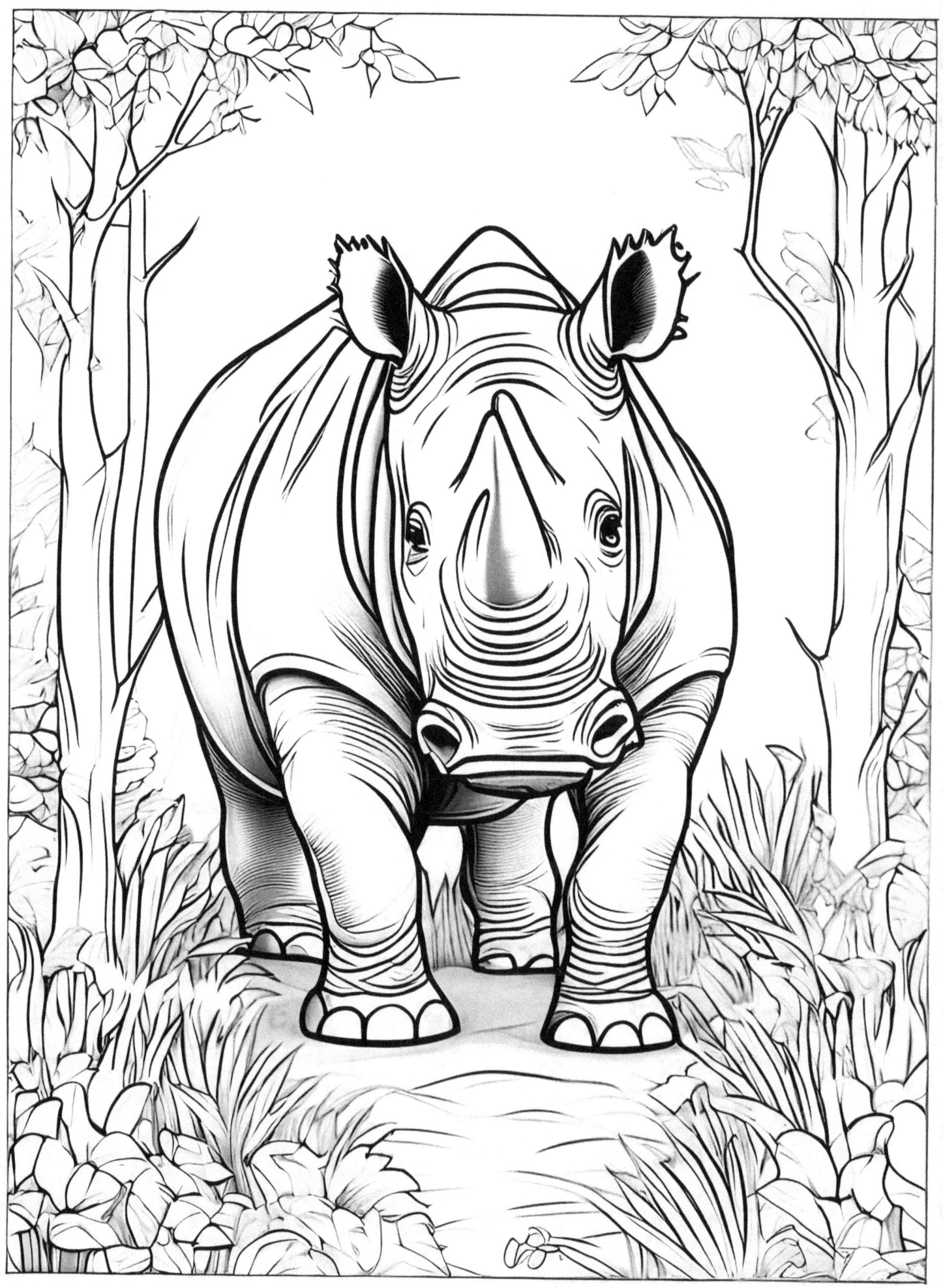

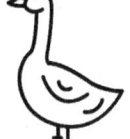

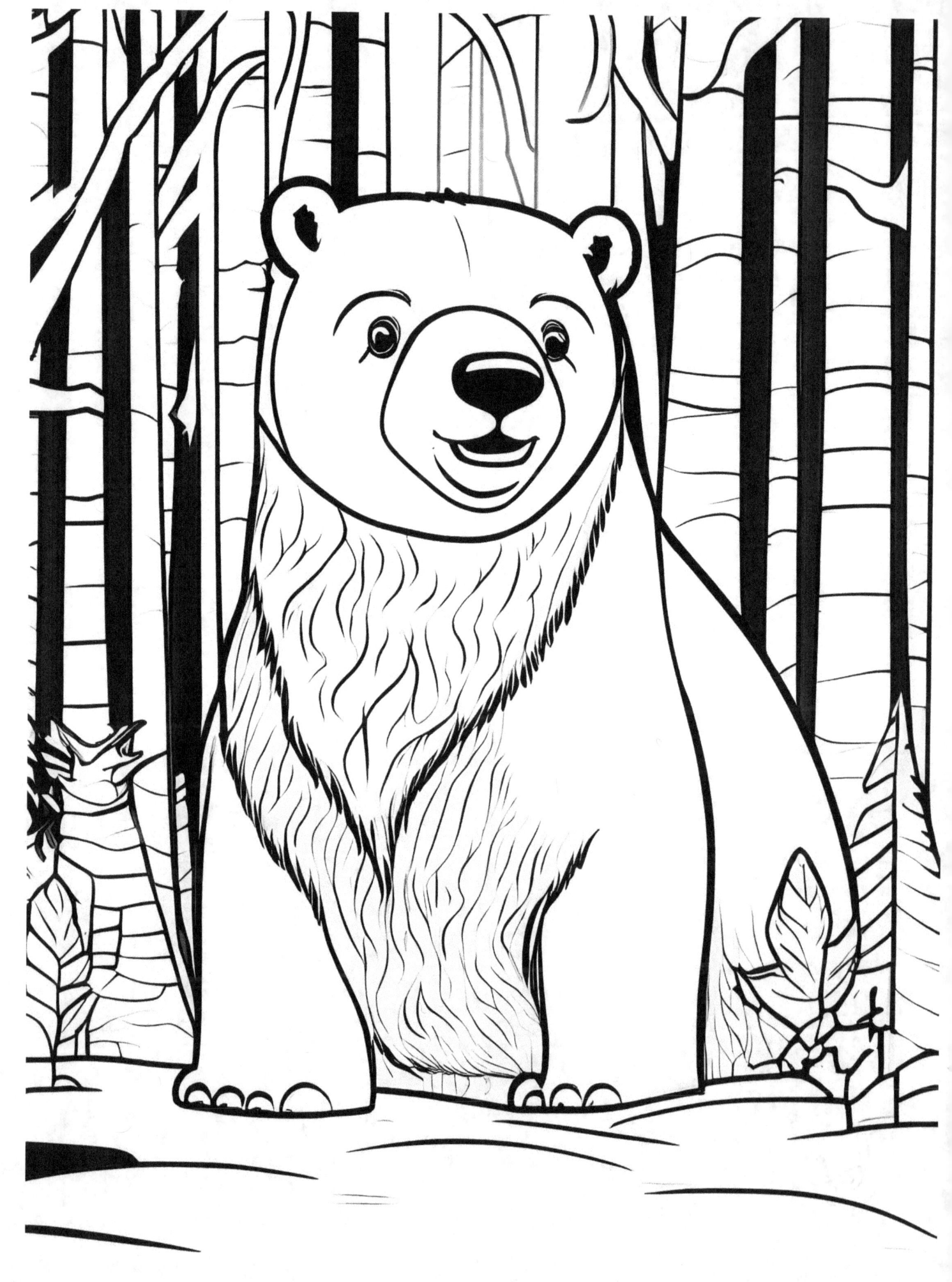

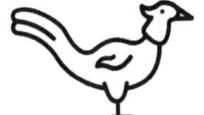

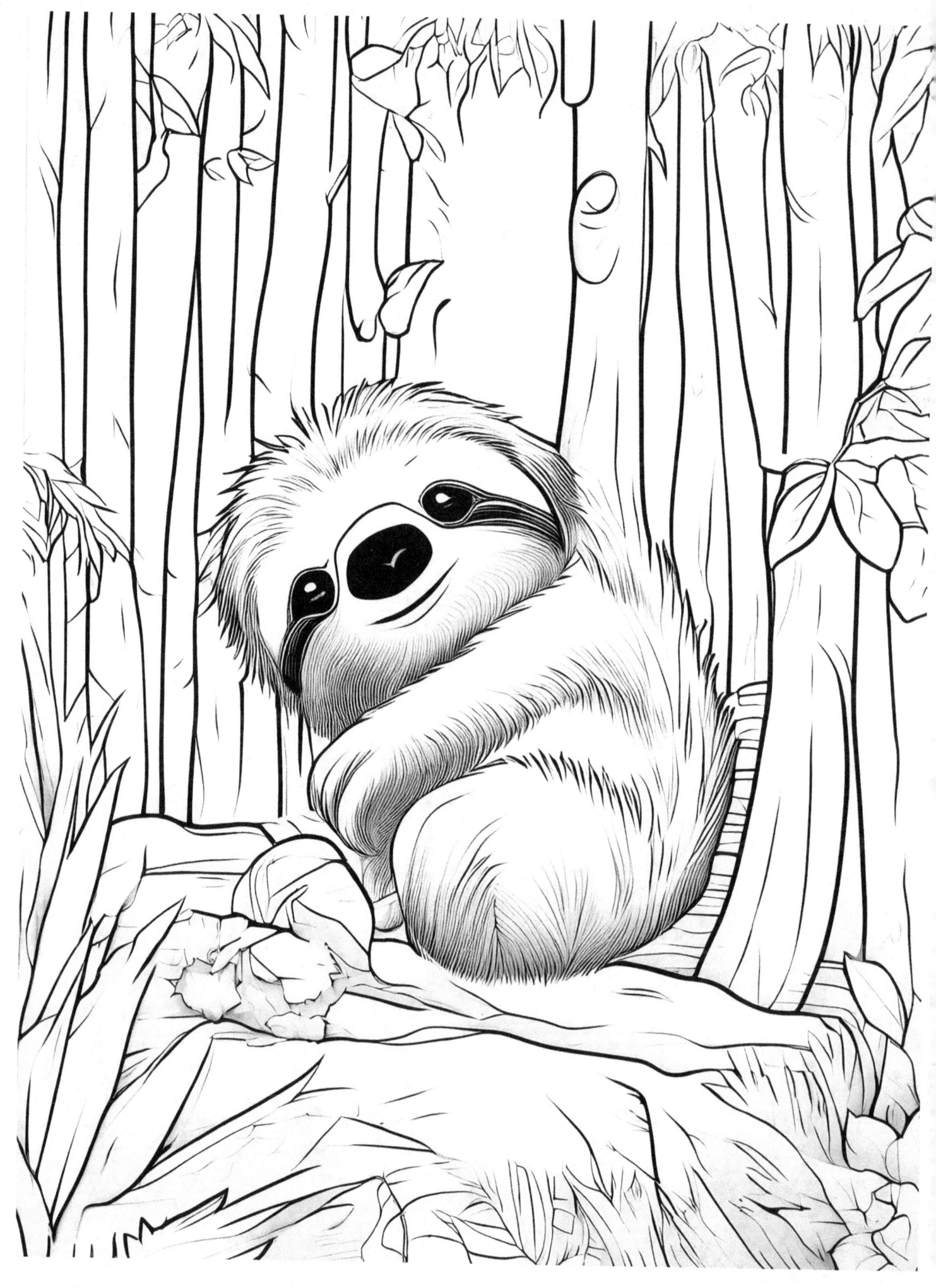

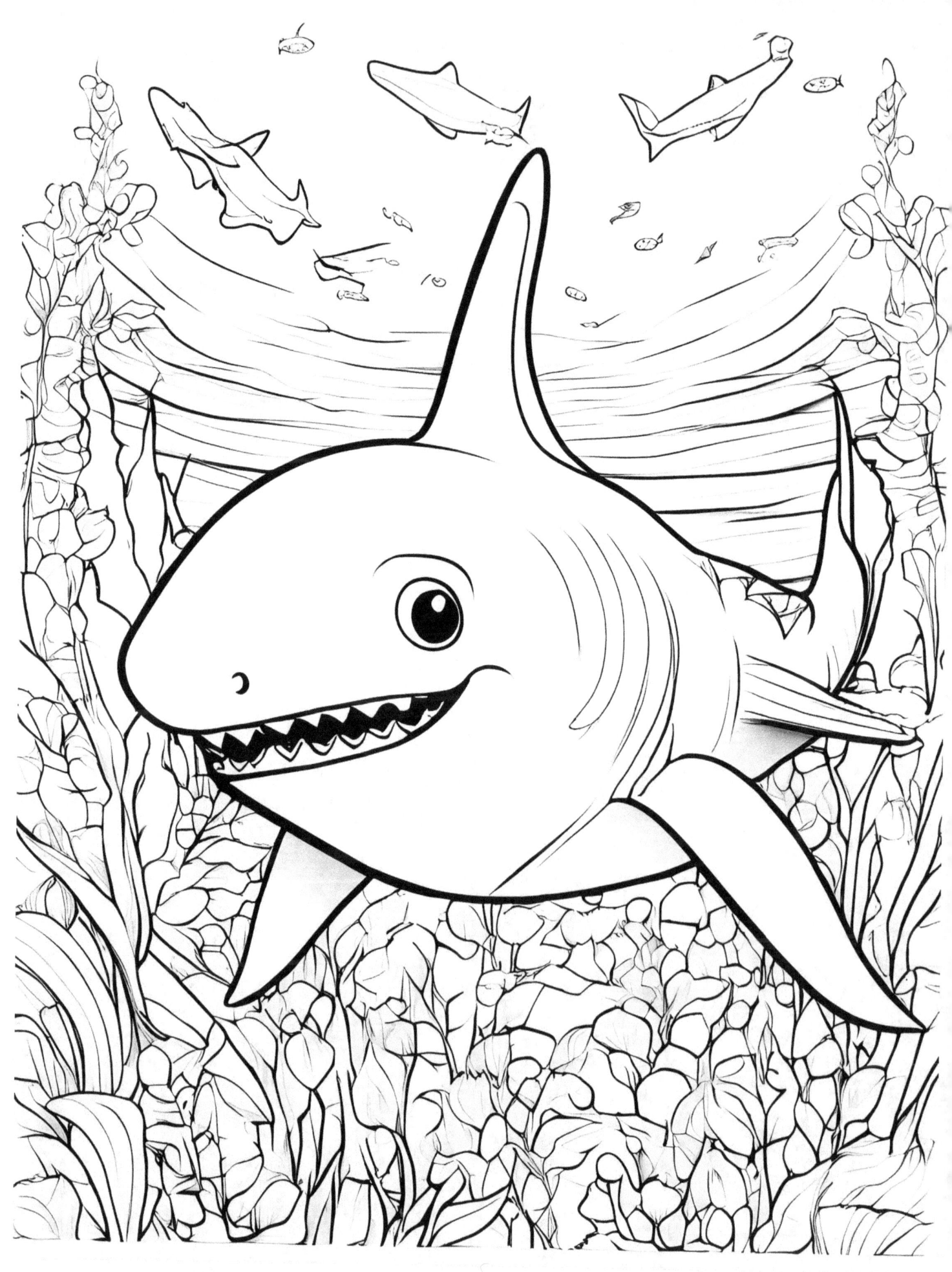

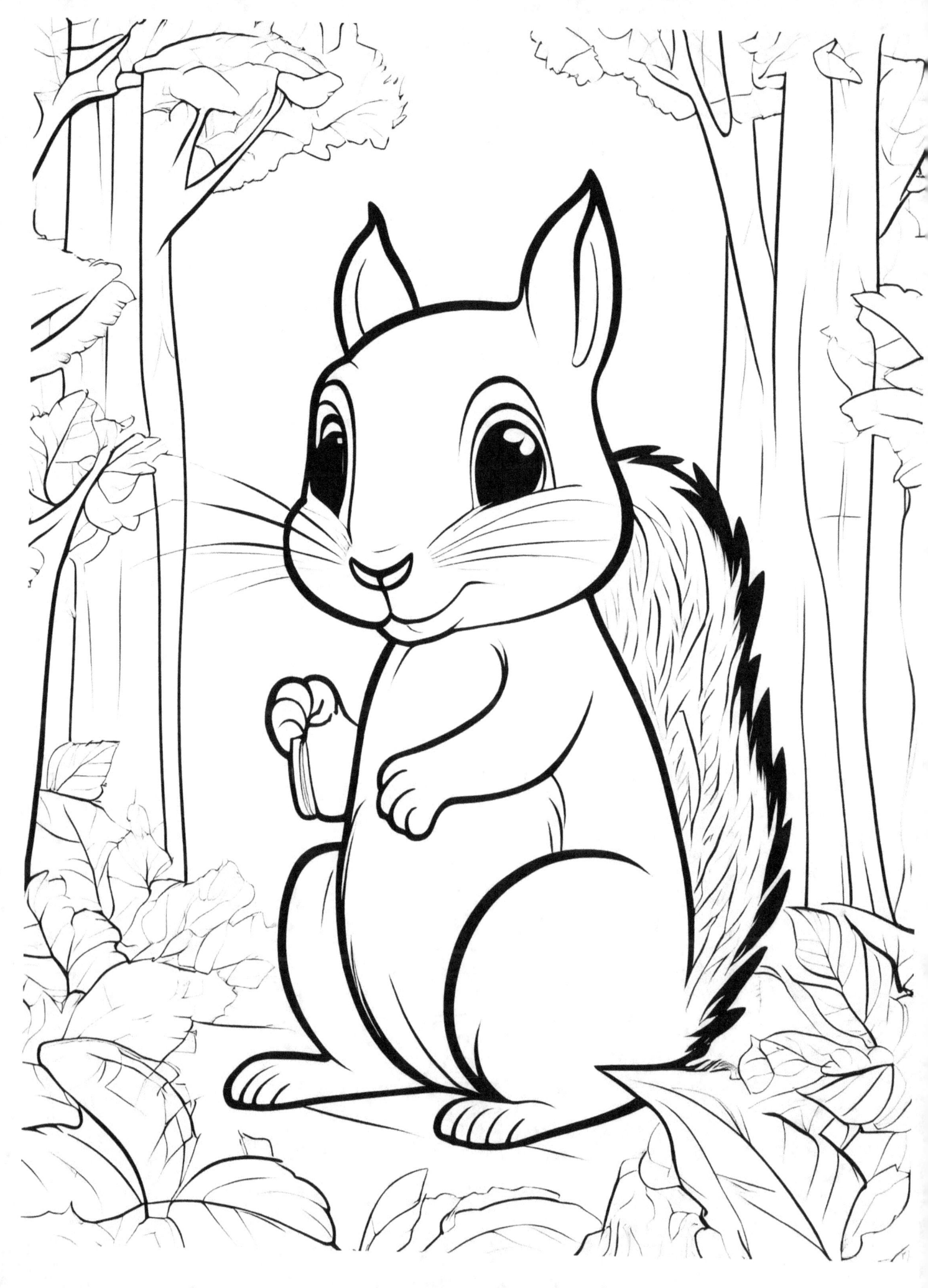

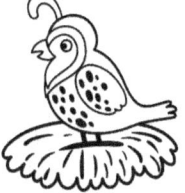

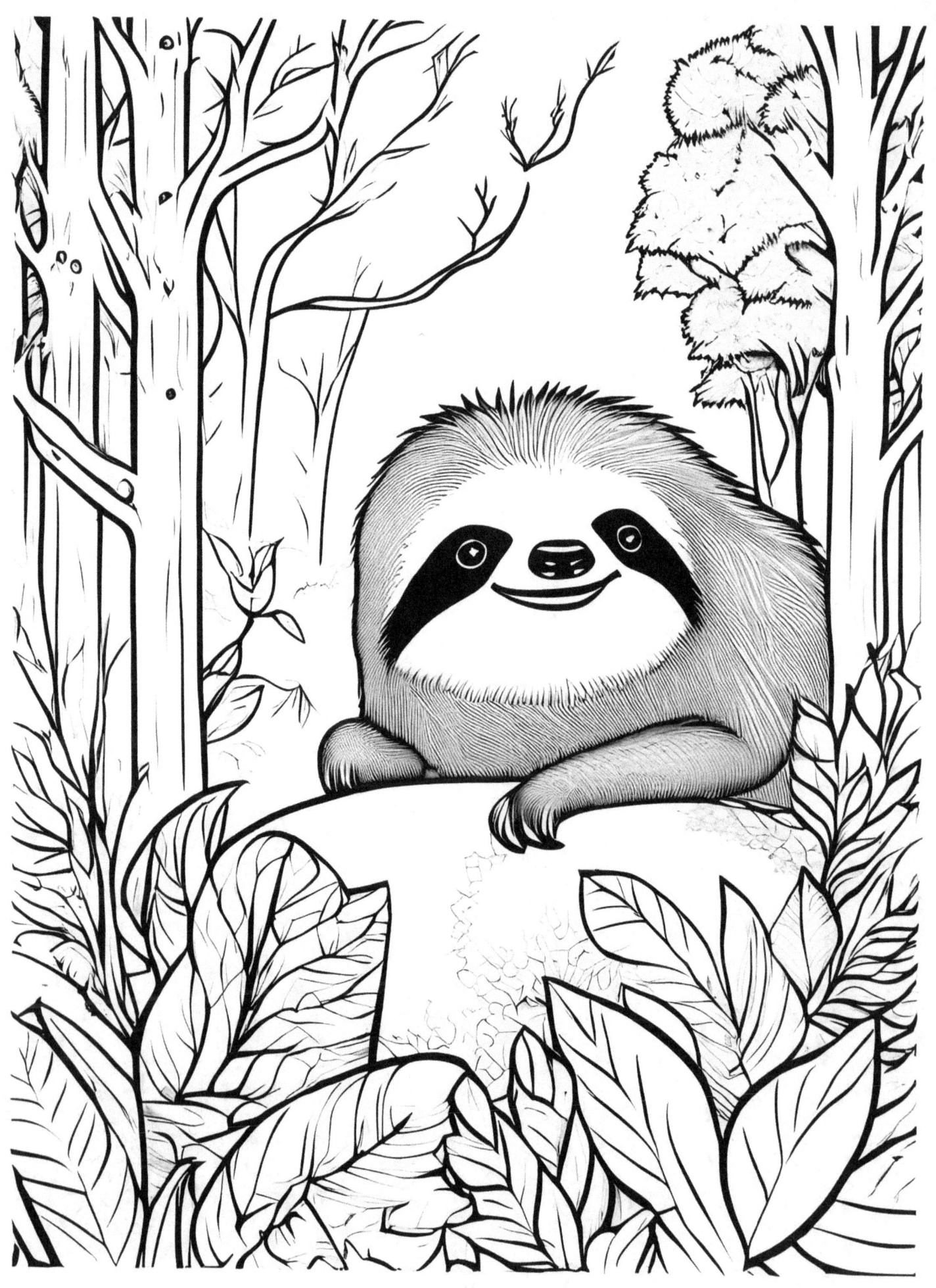

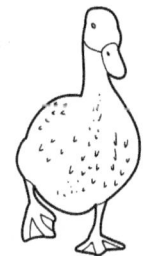

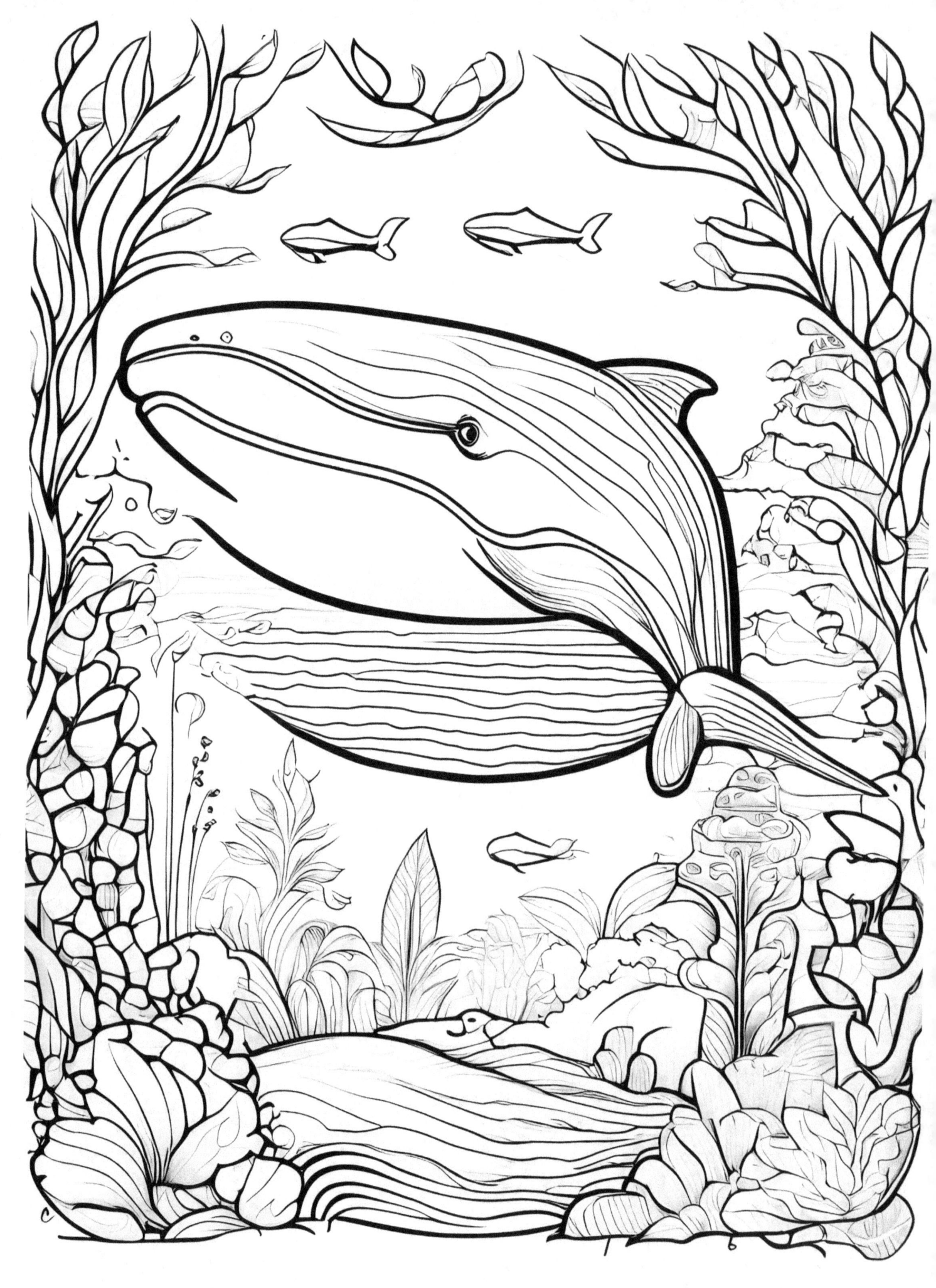